FROM ONE TO ONE THOUSAND HORSEPOWER

First published in 2004 by

WOODFIELD PUBLISHING
Bognor Regis, West Sussex, England
www.woodfieldpublishing.com

ISBN 1-903953-52-9

FROM ONE TO ONE THOUSAND HORSEPOWER

… or how a Scottish Cavalryman became a Spitfire pilot in World War II

FERGUS DAVIDSON

Woodfield

The Author in the uniform of the Scottish Horse Regiment.

With grateful thanks to

Margaret ~ my long-suffering wife, for her tolerance and patience during my 'brush with history'.

Neil and Jennifer ~ ever ready to assist in anything I needed to know or anywhere I wanted to go.

Doris Davidson ~ for her boundless enthusiasm and encouragement, not to mention her expertise.

Contents

The Author in the uniform of his second career as a police officer, Aberdeen Police HQ, 1976.

Introduction

There comes a time in a man's life when it dawns on him that he can remember almost every detail of what happened to him forty, fifty or sixty years ago and can't remember what he had for yesterday's dinner. The question now is… should he let time take its course and grow old with as much dignity as he can… or should he keep his brain active by jotting down his memories for the benefit of his children and grandchildren? Regretting not having found out more about my own parents' lives, I plumped for the latter, and once started, with the events of the thirties and forties crowding in upon me, some I had practically forgotten, some I wished I could forget – it occurred to me that my experiences, probably not all of them unique, were sufficiently unusual and diverse taken as a whole as to be of interest to others besides my immediate family and thus worth recording properly.

In setting this account down on paper I have described the sequence of events as they happened – some humorous and romantic, others tragic and gruelling, occasionally touching the very depths of despair. I have watered nothing down, even the encounters with imminent death, in an attempt to revisit the emotions I felt at the time.

All in all, I think I can claim a small degree of achievement and I hereby present my memoir *From One to One Thousand Horsepower* solely for the purpose of entertaining, amusing and perhaps assisting younger generations to understand the part their parents or grandparents played in the Second World War, and hopefully respect them for it.

I have endeavoured to maintain a reasonable level of historic and factual accuracy but if at any point in this narrative I should have failed in this respect I apologise, in advance, to the experts.

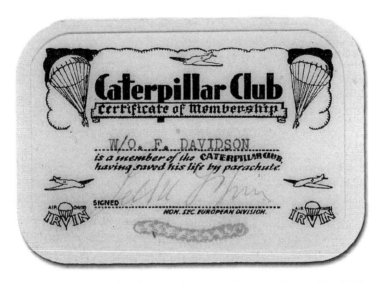

The Author's membership certificate for the Irvin Caterpillar Club exclusively for aviators whose lives have been saved by making a parachute jump.

EARLY DAYS

Author and pal on a cycling holiday.

Author on the salmon nets, Aberdeen.

SCHOOLDAYS & APPRENTICESHIP

In the early 1930s I was still at Mile End School[1] when I was given a model steam engine as a Christmas present. Let me make it quite clear that this was not a toy, but a fine example of model engineering, and I was completely bowled over by it. Most of my spare time was spent priming it with methylated spirits and putting a match to it, waiting with bated breath for the water in the little compartment to come to the boil and my engine to start puffing. It didn't go anywhere, of course, yet the knowledge that it *could* move if I had a track for it, and could even pull carriages if I possessed any, was enough to have me walking on cloud nine, and I set my heart on being an engineer some day.

But I was a child then, with other things to do, stupid things, like shinning up lampposts to put out the gas street lights. Crawling into the space under the row of cellars at the rear of the houses – a place frequented by 'wild' cats – didn't do much for a boy's jersey either, nor for his peace of mind, but it had to be done; it was the only way to become 'one of the gang'. Girls were accepted, most reluctantly, but only as nurses – no front line stuff. Unfortunately, during races, when one or two bodies had to be tripped up to provide casualties, the very occasional female patients attracted more attention than hitherto. Those soft bits!

But technology was soon taking over from boyish pranks. I had to accompany my dad one day to the Woodside area of

---

[1] classed as one of the best primaries (perhaps *the* best) in Aberdeen at the time and continuing to be so recognised for more than sixty years after that, but, sadly, in the early 21st century to be added to the long list of substantial granite buildings already demolished to make way for housing.

Aberdeen, about three miles from Mid Stocket. When we reached our destination, a bit of bargaining went on before a large pole was produced. I'd never seen anything like it. Although quite slender, it was at least 30 feet long and obviously very heavy, but having managed to load it on to a two-wheeled cart, we set off for home. The traffic was easier in those days, though we did run into difficulties. Our route was mostly downhill and we didn't have the luxury of disc brakes – or any type of brakes – and the cart had a mind of its own, trundling hither and yonder as it fancied. As you can imagine, this didn't exactly endear us to other users of the 'king's highway', nor do much for our own peace of mind.

We got home all in one piece, however, including our cargo which, with the assistance of some incredulous neighbours, was duly erected about 25 yards from the back of the house and attached to the side of a large shed occupied by Alexander Hall & Co., Joiners, who owned several of the properties in the area and who must have granted permission.

Mother was outraged by the sheer size of the pole.

'You said it was just to hold a wire,' she said, accusingly.

'And so it is!' she was told, in no uncertain manner by my harassed Dad.

You will probably have guessed that this was for a wireless aerial. I did say it was technology … a crystal set no less, with a cat's whisker which had to be located with unerring accuracy on a specific part of a crystal – if it was quartz, Seiko had not yet heard of it. It was a delicate operation, the slightest vibration had an adverse effect, but if the elusive kernel was found, a strange noise could be heard by the 'elite' – i.e. he who had the headphones, in other words, my father. Such was the success of the high wire antenna that intermittent screeches were known to come from a horn on the actual set. It wasn't Luxembourg, of course, but it *was* the BBC.

As always, entrepreneurs (in however small a way) have their set-backs, and my dad's came from a uniformed member of the General Post Office, who pointed out that our aerial was crossing over the telephone wire, and was therefore illegal. This correction was made with reluctance... but Authority had spoken.

Although this public address system had to be confined – reception on earphones was surprisingly good, even with wires from the kitchen to my bedroom. How he got the wires there, I don't know. This was the era of the Big Bands – 'This is Henry Hall speaking' – and other famous names including Joe Loss and Geraldo, plus all the latest news items ... fantastic! To lie in bed with the wireless and read Arthur Mee's *Children's Encyclopaedia* opened a new world for me.

Another part of growing up was delivering newspapers and 'butteries', also known as 'rowies' (delicious morning rolls which were, and still are, exclusive to Aberdeen and its environs). In this, I had a rival. He delivered rolls for Strathdee, the baker; I worked for Mitchell & Muil. He had the advantage of a bicycle, and with his accuracy in throwing bags of butteries at the doors while cycling along the pavement, there was no contest...at first. But as the days passed, I noticed that the amount of my deliveries was increasing as his diminished. Quality of service always counts!

I did eventually manage to coax my sister into lending me the bicycle she'd inherited from an aunt, Mrs Watt, whose engineer son was later to have a big influence on my life.

Among many happy cycling memories I clocked up as a young adventurer, a weekend at Forres with my chum features prominently for the lovely weather and bathing and swimming in rather chilly water. On one of our runs, we stumbled on what turned out to be a nesting place for Arctic terns. Any time we'd seen these birds before, we had got the impression that they were quite good humoured... but not when nesting! We retreated hastily to leave them in peace.

A few months later, in a race with a pal, going in opposite directions round some houses, the inevitable happened and we collided. My sister was furious, and it was a long time before I got another bike!

When I reached the Central Secondary School a year or so later, I was pleased to see Science in the timetable, and this was one class where each lesson just flew past and I could hardly wait for the next. I was fascinated by all aspects of the subject, the Bunsen burner in particular, and I was soon using my meagre pocket money to buy mercury instead of sweets. I also bought a glass tube, and, with the mercury, and entirely unaided, made a barometer. Floating on a cloud of pride at this achievement, I soon discovered that thermometers were more difficult, though a capillary tube could be sealed with heat and a bulb formed to hold the mercury. I did manage to produce one or two that were reasonably accurate, completely unaware, until many years later, of the dangers of the substances I was handling. As they say, ignorance is bliss.

I was still determined to work with engines when I grew up, so you can imagine what a young impressionable schoolboy such as I thought of Sandy Watt, the cousin who came home on leave from the Burma Oil Company around 1934 or 35. He was an absolute hero to me and I sat practically at his feet listening with eyes wide and heart racing as he told us of his exploits and the good social life there. 'This could be me,' I assured myself, ignoring any mention of the perils he often had to face.

'You know, John, there's great scope out there for engineers,' Sandy told my father one evening, sending my hopes sky-high, 'particularly if they're Scottish. They think there's nobody like us, even though some of my pals are inclined to let off a bit of steam now and then. Nothing too bad, of course, just high spirits after a hard day's work.'

At that time, Scotland was reputed to have the best education system in the whole world – it was said that a Scot held a prime post in every large concern in every country you could name. I doubt if the same holds true today. Our present education system leaves an awful lot to be desired.

An engineer himself, Sandy went on, 'I climbed the ladder quite fast, really, and I'm sure I got promoted mainly because I'd taken the trouble to learn the language. That goes down well in a foreign country.'

These were the hungry thirties, remember – when the men of Jarrow were joined by hundreds of others on their rebellious march to London – and such opportunities were not to be taken lightly. They were, in fact, very rare, almost impossible to get, and influenced by all this I made up my mind that if ever I got the same chance as my cousin I would grab it with both hands and follow his example. I would learn half a dozen languages, even Chinese or Greek if necessary; I would watch and absorb every detail of the job; I would work like a slave and never blot my copybook by drinking. That way, I'd reach the very top of the tree…

Ah, the naivety of youth!

I was quite happy at the Central, nevertheless I found myself mulling over the idea of leaving in order to further what, at that time, could only have been a boyish whim.

First of all – though, I can't for the life of me explain why, because it wasn't exactly a job that appealed to me, possibly just to make some money until I was old enough to get into engineering – I went for an interview in a chartered accountant's office in Union Terrace. Looking back on it now, with a lifetime of experience of this kind of thing, I don't think that the interviewer and I impressed each other all that much, so the least said about it the better. In any case, it was just as well that I wasn't successful there. I might have been a pen-pusher stuck behind a desk for the rest of my life.

Quite soon after this, I spotted an advert in the local evening paper and, with my parents' consent, I applied for work at John M. Henderson's, a well known firm of engineers in Aberdeen's King Street. The possibility of me getting an apprenticeship pleased my dad. He had always been in favour of me 'learning a trade'.

The interview in King's Works was with a Mr Walker – known irreverently, I was to discover later, as 'Baldie' for obvious reasons – who must have been quite satisfied with this particular youngster, because he referred me to Mr Marshall, the Works Manager, who pointed me in the right direction. I was accepted as an apprentice at a starting wage of 7/6 – yes, seven shillings and six pence (just over 37p in today's toy money) for a five and a half day week, rising by annual increments to 15/- (fifteen shillings, or 75p today).

I was delighted! With money in my pocket, I would be able to buy what *I* wanted, not what my mother thought was good for me, and I was itching to use one of the machines that stood outside some of the shops. You had to put in one penny (an *old* penny, worth less than half the *new* penny) and out would come a paper packet holding five Woodbines and a few matches. I would feel like a man!

No, I *was* a man! At fifteen, I was grown-up!

OFF TO WORK

On my first day at work, I was introduced to the South Shop, a vast, noisy place, where the larger structures were assembled. I began to learn that from here, cranes, cableways and winches were sent to many parts of the world, but mostly to Africa. A section known as 'the Corner' was set aside as a machine shop for milling, planing and other such delicate operations in the charge of Willie Strachan, a topper of a chap, especially when dealing with 'youngsters'. I was given limited responsibility and I noticed that none of the items I was dealing with would have been very expensive to replace because they were flawed, although the word the men used for them was 'poxed'.

I liked the atmosphere, but as in all such firms, there were capers, tricks played on apprentices and the unwary, and I was at the bottom of the heap, the newest boy, ripe for teasing. Tools had a habit of disappearing, and an oil-soaked rag could come at me occasionally out of nowhere, but it was all done, and received, in good humour. Only on one occasion can I remember tempers fraying.

My tormentor's name was Hyland, and I can't remember what he did to get my dander up – maybe it was an argument that went wrong. It couldn't have been that bad otherwise it would be engraved in my memory, but at the time, I considered that he was going too far and I had to retaliate. He was asking for a fight and I obliged. Simple! Anyway, the contretemps ended when I clattered his head against a vice. We weren't reprimanded in any way; in fact I think the onlookers were on my side. They likely shared my view that Hyland shouldn't have picked on me – he was bigger than I was.

I eventually graduated from what might be termed the kindergarten into the main shop. On looking back, I recall this area as being dominated by a large guillotine, a fearsome instrument made by Pels of Germany, which could cut absolutely anything. I was now being 'put on' with various journeymen to further my education, picking something up from each one that would stand me in good stead as an engineer.

If I recall correctly, the wage of a time-served engineer at that time was about £3 per week, and working overtime was the only way to augment this, as far as I knew – doing 'homers' on a twenty-ton crane would have been a bit difficult.

The usual procedure was that the foreman would come round with a smile on his face, a rather rare sight. 'Work tonight, boys?' he would say. It was an order, of course, not a question, and woe betide any man who didn't fall in with it. Not that I know of many who refused. It was, however, optional for boys in the early stages of their apprenticeship.

The evening work meant carrying on past the usual stopping time of five thirty-six until nine o'clock, and I suppose, in those early days, I felt obliged to do so out of a sense of loyalty to the men, because I knew they were happy about the extra money they'd earn. Overtime, of course, also meant taking a 'piece' which was made up when home for dinner, that is, if you went home in the middle of the day, or brought with you in the morning if you didn't. What did I get for these three extra hours? Well may you ask! My remuneration was the magnificent sum of sixpence, which did little more than pay for my refreshment between 5.37 p.m. and 6 p.m., which was usually a meat sandwich and a flask of tea. Still, it was all experience – part of training to be a working man.

On other occasions, if the overtime was to be more arduous, it was usually anticipated, because it would have been made known earlier in the week that whatever we were working on was scheduled to go out on the Saturday. This called for working through the Friday night until noon the following day, quite a substantial number of hours at time-and-a-quarter, maybe time-and-a-half for some – only Sundays merited double time and it had to be *essential!*

Of course, on the next pay day I could hear the men bewailing the amount of income tax that had been deducted from their wages – 'It's hardly worth working a' nicht when the tax man tak's half,' they would grumble. But they didn't refuse the chance the next time it came up. I was lucky. I didn't have to pay tax on the overtime I was paid.

I clearly remember one Saturday after working straight through from Friday teatime. A formidable piece of heavy machinery was being lowered from the overhead crane into a stout wooden packing case when it was noticed that the packer was actually still in the crate, making sure that there were no bits of metal or other foreign bodies present that could damage the contents. There were screams of 'Stop, stop!' The power was immediately switched off...but the load kept coming down. The solenoid brake, doing its best to obey the sudden shutdown, laboured and squealed in protest, as if about to blow-up. I'm not given to exaggeration, but I swear that when it finally stopped, it was only a few feet from the terrified man's head. This near-tragedy, of course, would never have happened if we hadn't all been half-asleep on our feet. Such a situation wouldn't be tolerated today.

On a lighter note, during another overnight stint it was noticed that a turner (lathe operator) had nodded off. I was delegated to paint his boots white, an accepted prank played on slumbering workers, and I was making quite a good job of it when the slumberer awoke. I took to my heels... but so did he, his speed in no way retarded by the tin he had picked up. A thump on the back brought me to a halt, and wondering what had hit me, I became conscious of a strong smell of paint. The victim had taken his revenge by flinging the tin at me, but all I could do was stare in horror at the mess on the boiler suit my mother had recently bought at the Co-op, a not inexpensive item. What would she say when she saw it now?

My conspirators had vanished. I was in a fix, but I did know that the paint store was quite near at hand. Turpentine, that's what was needed, and lots of it. Some paint did come off, but not before my boiler suit, not to mention my trousers, were soaked. At first, it was just annoyingly itchy, then it became most uncomfortable, even painful. They had to come off!

Shortly after this, to add to my distress, I discovered that my trousers had vanished during an unguarded moment. I wasn't kept long in ignorance, thank goodness. Someone, probably not the culprit, took pity on me and said they'd been tied to the flagpole on the roof – at least seventy feet from the ground! A kindly soul relented, however, and had them taken down, but not before I'd witnessed the spectacle of my 'breeks' billowing in the wind in full view of all the workers and, no doubt, grinning tram passengers with their noses glued to the windows. It would have been worse had it been during the day, of course, so I suppose I should have counted myself lucky.

Happy days? Yes, they were! Despite the ribbings, the teasings, the hard work and extra overtime; despite the iciness in those huge sheds in the winters, when hands turned blue with the cold, cement floors deprived feet of all feeling and we had sympathy for all brass monkeys; despite the sweltering heat in the summers, when 'semmits' stuck to backs and the sweat dripped off noses. Despite all that, I still look back on them with fondness. What I classed as hardships at the time were as nothing compared to what I was to endure in later years.

An apprenticeship then was something to be proud of, a case of being taught by men who knew their trade inside out, and who, although they stood no nonsense and could be severe if there was any sign of slackness, could make a young lad feel he was doing something worthwhile. Of course, he also grew up in the same mould as his tutors, but this was no bad thing. Most of them were good men, fine examples.

I had gained some very valuable experience with a 'ganger' by the name of Jock Anderson, when he asked me one day, out of the blue, 'How'd you like to come on a journey wi' me, laddie?'

Not knowing whether or not he was being serious, I hedged, 'Where to?'

'You ken the crane the squad's just finished? Well, it's for Thornhill Power Station, and I've to go there to set it up, but I need some help, see? And it strikes me you'd be the best lad for the job, you kenning how I work, like.'

This could almost have been a compliment, a pat on the back, but I was still a bit wary. 'Aye, Jock, I see what you mean, but where's this Thornhill Power Station?' For all I knew it could have been on the moon.

'Ach, did they nae learn you onything at the school? It's near Dewsbury, and afore you ask, Dewsbury's in Yorkshire, and Yorkshire's in...'

'...in the north of England,' I snapped, stung by his assumption that I didn't even know that. I'd been at the Central, for goodness sake, a secondary school!

'Well, then, how's about it? Will you come? It'll be a fine change for you, and it's nae something you'll get a chance at often.'

I was well aware of that, but I'd never been far from Aberdeen before, and the prospect of leaving Scotland altogether was a bit daunting. 'I'll need to ask my mother first.'

I'd half expected him to sneer about me being tied to her apron strings, but he just nodded. 'Right you are, but you'll let me ken once you come back from your dinner, eh?'

Timid though I was, the idea of going on such a long trip and then actually helping to erect one of Henderson's massive cranes was growing more attractive by the minute, so I raced home in great excitement to beg my mother to let me go.

While I hurried up Rosemount Place, something one of the engineers had once told me popped into my mind. It concerned a former employee, a one-eyed ganger called Sinclair who had been working in Africa, in charge of an erection job with only the natives to assist him. Not trusting them to work unsupervised, if he had to be absent from the site for any reason, he left his artificial eye in a prominent place as an 'overseer'... and it worked! 'But we wouldn't have a problem like that,' I assured myself. The people of Dewsbury – Dewsburghers? Dewsburians? – weren't 'natives' they were 100% British and would be completely reliable. And so they turned out to be.

But I digress. Back to Jock Anderson, a rather surly individual, quite small but potent, and with my parental permission confirmed he set arrangements in motion for me to accompany him the following day, Saturday – my first time really away from home. I don't think I slept a wink that night, I was so keyed up.

Not knowing how long the job would take, my mother had packed nearly all the clothes I possessed into an old travelling bag, or maybe it was called a valise, I'm not sure. She made me take a bath in the afternoon to be sure that every inch of me was clean in case I met with an accident on my travels – you know how mothers are, always looking on the black side. But even that couldn't dampen my enthusiasm.

The London train was due to leave Aberdeen at 6.10 p.m., and I was there in good time, at least half-an-hour before I needed to be, standing on the platform somewhat apprehensively with full kit. 6.05 and no Jock! I could see my wonderful trip disappearing into thin air and my knees were starting to tremble when he turned up… very drunk. I'm proud to say I didn't panic. I had, literally, to carry him onto the train. I was to carry him quite a lot on that expedition!

I fell asleep after a while and awoke at a station that I believed to be York, so I roused Jock from his slumber and dragged him and his baggage onto the platform. Unfortunately, it wasn't York – it was Grantham! I was thankful that he wasn't a violent man, but he certainly was vociferous, strings of angry words flowing from his mouth, but nothing my mother would have been horrified at, just mild oaths and variations on 'You silly boy!' as Captain Mainwaring was to say in 'Dad's Army' many years later, though I must admit, a wee bit stronger. Luckily, a long-suffering guard heard the rumpus and realising what had happened, took pity on me. With his help, I managed to get the outraged Jock back on board the train and we continued on to York and eventually, Dewsbury.

We got digs quite near the Power Station, which saved us having to walk any distance to work. We were ushered into a nicely-furnished front room by a rather elderly, grey-haired gent by the name of Hepburn. I can't speak for my travelling companion, but at my age, I was quite taken aback by the sight of a much younger woman (who turned out to be Mrs Hepburn) sitting on a chair by the fire with a baby at a voluptuous breast. But they were friendly folk, or to be perfectly honest, *she* was the friendlier, a bit too friendly for my liking. Tea in bed in the early morning was very acceptable, and I wasn't too bothered by the saucy stories that came with it, but it was a different matter when I realised that I was expected to move over. Maybe I was tempted – it was too long ago to re-call my exact feelings – but I didn't oblige, I do remember that.

Our evenings were free and while I was in a cinema one night the picture was interrupted by a broadcast saying that King Edward VIII had abdicated. I suppose this was momen-tous news really, a truly historic event, but it wouldn't affect me to any great extent. I couldn't see that it would make any difference at all. He hadn't been King for more than a few months anyway, and his brother would probably be able to do the job just as well. (He did, didn't he? Probably better.)

Accompanying Jock on one of his regular visits to the Black Bull seemed to make me a target for the scantily-dressed showgirl who was determined to sit on my knee, though I must have looked rather immature to her... which I was, of course! I wouldn't have been so embarrassed if I'd been a couple of years older; I'd likely have taken full advantage of the situation! One of the many missed opportunities of my youth...

Assisted by local labour, it took us three months to com-plete and test the crane, which was to be used to unload coal from barges in the nearby canal. Any further work that might be needed was to be carried out by men already employed on the site, so Jock and I were free to come home.

While we were in Dewsbury, I had often acted as my men-tor's 'minder', to use a more modern expression, seeing him back to our lodgings, jollying him out of his many 'mornings-after', but I still respected him. No matter how much of a hang-over he was suffering from, he knew precisely what had to be done and never made one single error in judgement. Men of his calibre are few and far between nowadays.

VENTURING FURTHER AFIELD

A trip to Grays in Essex, to dismantle a cantilever steam crane and erect it on the south breakwater at Aberdeen, was another of my expeditions. After we had made it ready for transportation, it was sent on its long journey north, its purpose being the reinforcing of the breakwater with twenty-ton concrete blocks. On its arrival in the city, a squad of seven of Hendersons' engineers, all good men, worked virtually round the clock for three months to complete it before the coming of the winter gales.

When *they* blast in from the north and you're in a place that's open to the elements you need to hold onto something substantial with both hands to avoid being blown off your feet. A breakwater, I can assure you, is no place to be at times like that, and besides, all engineers, no matter how skilled they may be, need the use of two hands to do their job properly. There are sometimes severe gales in autumn and spring as well, of course, and conditions in the north-east coast of Scotland can be quite fearsome even in summer.

One day, with the promise of an afternoon off, I was dared to jump into the sea beyond the rocks, and not wanting the time-served men to say I was scared, I accepted the dare. I jumped in! In nothing but my underpants! Older and wiser, I hope, I don't for a minute think that they seriously meant me to do it, but I can still remember the shock of entering the icy waters and fighting for breath as they closed in over my head. Naturally, my fellow workers, looking somewhat shocked themselves, pulled me out straight away, and, thankfully, I still had dry clothes to put on again. I didn't tell either of my parents of that little episode.

My financial circumstances as an apprentice meant that most of my leisure time was spent at home – time was practically all I had to spend. My dad, a baker to trade, was in steady employment as was my sister Ellen, three years my senior. Our gas-lit flat was on the top floor of a tenement at 16 Mid Stocket Road, a free-standing granite building erected in late or mid Victorian times and set back off the road. This block began the street proper, then came an unbroken line of slightly newer tenements until they reached Mile End Avenue. Some way farther on from there, the tenements gave way to two-storeyed, one tenanted houses, which in turn, were followed on in the thirties by detached and semi-detached villas.

To return to what I was saying before I got side-tracked, let me make it quite clear that my childhood home was a happy one, and with many of my pals living nearby, I was never at a loss for company. We had few of the home comforts that are commonplace today, but we were none the worse for that. There was a communal wash-house at the rear of our building, with the usual wooden tubs, and washday meant Mother rising about 6 a.m. to get the fire going under the boiler, then awkwardly manoeuvring her mangle from our cellar, twenty yards away. It was on castors, not the roller-balls of today, but creaky devils of things, stiff and awkward and determined to go their own way, so it took some effort to trundle such a weight even that short distance along a beaten, uneven path.

The drying green was spacious and, of course, each family had its allocated 'day'. With six tenants in the building, only Sundays were clear, and quite rightly, for they were looked on as sacrosanct. 'Thou shalt do no washing on the Sabbath,' might have been the eleventh commandment. Anyone ignoring this was regarded as a heathen, or, just as bad in the Presbyterian minds of the women of the twenties and thirties, an atheist. God knows what they'd have thought of the flapping clothes-lines peppering all areas of the city every Sunday in these degenerate times, even in the – ssh! – West End. There's no escaping the fact that tumble dryers don't leave the clothes with the lovely smell of fresh air, not even if the popular manufactured substitutes are used.

A row of lavatories extended from the wash-house, the most distant (ours, of course) being so far away that it meant a full-out sprint down several flights of stairs and the whole length of the back-yard if we were desperate, or if we were *frantically* desperate, a slow, very careful walk with legs gripped tightly together in case such haste might precipitate an 'accident'. It took a tremendous effort of will to make the WC the final port of call in the dark, cold nights, particularly if the weather was bad, but it had to be done, even if the rain was lashing down, even if we couldn't see where we were going in a blizzard and had to feel our way along, counting other people's lavatory doors.

There was also the matter of keeping ourselves clean. With no bathroom, it meant washing at the kitchen sink and going to the public baths. Quite possibly, being brought up in such an environment was good for us, training us for the rigours of the life that was to come.

Not quite so terrible, just annoying, was the fact that bad weather on a washing day also meant a clothes horse being put up in the kitchen, straddling the fireside and blocking out the heat, which did little to cheer the place up. This affected me most when I was still at school and had to do my home-work at the far side of the table, in the direct line of the draught that swirled in from under the kitchen door.

You will have gathered that, no matter how Spartan the sur-roundings, I still recall No.16 with great affection, but sadly, it was pulled down in the sixties. At first, I thought that its position, breaking up the symmetry, must have offended some VIP's eye, so I could scarcely believe it when it was replaced by... a garage! Not a small, private garage, a proper, large garage with petrol pumps and all the other items essential to such an establishment; plus, of course, a steady stream of cars and tooting of horns to summon attention. To my mind, it was more out of place than the original tenement.

I have no idea whether the tenants of the surrounding houses complained, or if the same VIP's eye was offended anew, but the garage lasted only a few years before it also bit the dust. The 'block of flats' (not a tenement, for goodness sake) now standing there wasn't built with the original granite, the stone once used for all building in Aberdeen and which gave rise to its title 'the Silver City', but with brick-like imitations.

That first part of Mid Stocket Road has lost its character, though I suppose it won't be long before there will be nobody left to remember it as it once was.

From where we lived, the street climbed steadily to what was originally the Forest of Stocket – gifted to the city by King Robert the Bruce around the 14th century in gratitude for support given to his army – before levelling out into the open countryside, where we used to rove around as youths. Its summit today, however, leads to several housing estates, and you have to travel some miles before coming to the current city boundary. Instead of being on the outer edge of the outskirts as I remember it, Mid Stocket is now regarded as part of the city centre.

I was about sixteen, perhaps seventeen, when matters other than engines were brought to my attention. Marshall, my closest friend and the same age, was being 'sought after' by a girl called Kathleen who worked in a shop in George Street. He was always very neat and more than tidy, in fact, an all-round nice-looking lad… unlike myself. It seems that Kathleen had talked her friend into taking a walk up Queen's Road in the hope of seeing Marshal, as this was one of our favourite Sunday strolls – more relaxing than 'walking the mat', the term given to going up and down Union Street, *the* 'picker-up' of places.

My first impression of Kathleen, even from a distance, was that she was quite a hefty lass, but… her friend! Wow! Not only did she have a perfect figure, she was gorgeous, absolutely beautiful, with lovely black hair and dancing brown eyes. Kathleen introduced her as Margaret Mackay and I was delighted to learn that she lived in Rosemount Place, not all that far from Mid Stocket Road. For the very first time, something stirred in me, something I'd never felt before, unsettling but nice. I felt quite guilty about it, but there it was, the first glimmerings of an emotion I couldn't yet put a name to. We met only a few times and she told me long afterwards – a lifetime afterwards – that I hadn't made a great impression on her. Apparently, I'd spent most of the time reciting Burns' poetry – not a normally accepted method of courting!

On reflection, I suppose I was rather awkward, or maybe introspective, or perhaps just trying to show off my knowledge of our national poet. It wasn't surprising, then, that I made little progress with her, although I might have done if I'd had a bit more gumption and hadn't been so inexperienced. To let you understand, we were out for a run on our bikes one evening and stopped for a breather. Margaret was wearing shorts – the old-fashioned khaki kind, loose and reaching the knees, not the modern cropped version – and the sight of her shapely calves and about half-an-inch of shapely thigh – not often seen under the long skirts girls wore then – was too much for me. I grabbed at a knee, but it was to be many event-filled years before I got a chance to grab at the other. The sins of the

flesh went only so far, in those days... though there were ex-
ceptions. At that time mothers dinned into their sons that it
was wrong to touch the opposite sex until they were married
(how times have changed!) and into their daughters that no
decent boy would lay a finger on them until after the wedding
– which well-meant advice wasn't always observed.

Margaret and I had both been brought up to this belief,
and so, not finding much in common with each other apart
from the pull of attraction, we parted friends, but maybe I
wanted to be bosom friends even then?

A moving picture showing about this time also had a lasting
effect on me – *Hell's Angels*, with Ben Lyon as the hero and
Jean Harlow as the *femme fatale*; not that I paid much attention to them. What enthralled me were the winged vehicles
that soared across the sky, climbing, swooping... I'd never
seen anything like it, and I marvelled at the ability of man to
build and fly such superb machines. I cut out pictures of all
kinds of aeroplanes, I followed accounts in the newspapers of
the prizes offered for flights across the Atlantic, for solo flights
from America to Britain, and now, alongside my ambition to
be an engineer overseas, I set my heart on being a pilot some
day. I know that millions of youngsters cherished this dream,
but I was to be lucky! My dream came true.

As the thirties progressed, there were rumblings in Europe
and a German airship actually passed over Britain. All sorts of
sinister interpretations were being attributed to this, especially
because of a Music-Hall-type character called Adolf Hitler,
who seemed to have hypnotised the whole of Germany and
was now doing his best to annex as many of its neighbouring
countries as he could.

I didn't have much time to take in all the implications of
this. There was a new driving force at work. Orders, particularly defence-orientated, were flooding into Hendersons, and

to all the engineering works throughout Britain, I've no doubt. There was an upturn in the economy, an air of prosperity, although it was becoming obvious that war clouds were gathering.

Regrettably, the age of steam was slipping away. Steam driven engines were quite expensive to produce and required a high degree of expertise to build. Nor did they lend themselves to mass production. It was uncompetitive in the modern world. The electric motor had long since taken over.

In February 1938, tragedy struck my family. My father was taken into hospital for an operation to contain a rupture and, at first, he seemed to be progressing favourably, but only ten days later, a clot of blood from the wound reached his heart. His death had a disastrous effect on all of us, my mother and sister were devastated, and I, selfishly, even more so because it put an end to any hope of my ever going to India.

Rumours of war became even more foreboding, but because I was now involved in evening classes as well as my daytime work, I paid little heed. The engineering course for the National Certificate was not an easy one, so it was 'how' by day for me, and 'why' at the College.

In the outside world, one of the popular songs was *'I'm Happy When I'm Hiking,'* and further to that, there was much emphasis on physical fitness. The Keep Fit programme would – very shortly although we had no idea of what lay in front of us – stand us in good stead when it came to filling sand-bags, digging allotments… or trenches.

Another popular adage of the time was 'For an A1 nation, beer is best'. Unfortunately, while we drank it, Adolf was invading the Sudetenland and Austria and 'Mein Kampf' was being unfolded, digested and debated. It was beyond belief that its contents were anything but fantasies.

It was in this environment that Alfie, a schoolboy pal, sprung a wee surprise on me on our way home one night. 'D'you think Hitler'll try to invade us?' he began, digging a wayward chip out of the corner of his poke and running it round the paper to soak up every vestige of salt and vinegar.

We were often tempted into the 'chipper' by the more-than-appetising smell wafting out. We considered the small paper bag we got, filled to overflowing with delicious chipped potatoes, cooked as only Italians knew how, well worth the penny we had to hand over. Sadly, the art has been lost, and even if you pay fifty pence chips don't taste like they used to.

'Looks awful like it,' I nodded, turning my poke inside out and licking the moisture still remaining, before I pushed the paper down a brander in the gutter.

'I've been thinking…' Alfie murmured, sucking his fingers.

He paused and I waited. He was inclined to do this to me, rouse my curiosity and then expect me to ask what he was on about, but I wasn't going to oblige this time.

'The lad next door to me was telling me he's joined the Gordons,' he said at last. 'Well, the T.A., you know, the Terriers? He says it's great, and I was wondering…'

I didn't need to hear any more. 'Aye, it might be a good idea for us, and all. We should get involved. If it does come to war between us and Germany, we'd be ready for anything Hitler tries.'

Alfie nodded. 'That's what I thought, so I'm going to join tomorrow in my dinner hour. Are you game?'

'I'll think about it.' I was convinced that it was the right thing to do, but I didn't like it being sprung on me like that. Alfie'd had time to think it over.

I gave his suggestion a good deal of thought that night. Great publicity was being given to the activities of University Air Squadrons (which would have been the ideal answer for me if only I'd been at University) and the Royal Navy Reserve, as well as the Territorial Army, etc. You name it, it was available, even for women. I didn't fancy the Navy, so it would have to be the Army, and being Aberdonians the obvious choice for us was the Gordon Highlanders, the city's own (regrettably, in the 1990s integrated with several other long-standing Scottish regiments as just 'The Highlanders'). At that time, however, they were known far and wide for their fearlessness in every campaign they had ever fought, so I decided to enlist with Alfie.

Things, however, didn't quite go as planned...

. For one thing, I didn't get a full dinner hour the following day, and so it was Saturday afternoon before I was able to make my commitment... on my own, as Alfie had done on the Friday. When I turned up at the Drill Hall in Aberdeen's Woolmanhill – in the heart of the city and not an altogether salubrious area in those days (unrecognisable today, most of it turned into roundabouts and junctions that totally confuse motorists and terrify pedestrians) I was confronted by a person I took to be a recruiting sergeant, resplendent in red sash. You may think that this would have made me hasten to accept the King's shilling and fire me with the ambition to equal or better this man's rank some day, but he was anything but a good advertisement for his regiment.

To put it politely, he was under the 'affluence of incohol', as good old Will Fyfe used to say in his patter between choruses of '*I Belong to Glasgow*'. The modern expression would be 'pissed as a newt', but at the time, I could only describe him as being very drunk.

Sadly disillusioned, I retreated and stood outside, wondering what I should do, but, even sixty-odd years ago lads in their teens didn't take long to recover. There were other military establishments I could try. Within half an hour, I presented myself at Great Western Road – then, as now, a quiet street in the West End – and offered my services to 'B' Squadron of the Scottish Horse Territorial Army. It wasn't long before I was kitted out with breeches and spurs – the order of the day for a cavalry regiment – and attending 'drills'. Maybe it was my acquaintanceship with a horse while on a holiday at Kemnay that prompted this choice.

But there was more – so much more. They hired horses from a local stable, and I, city born and bred, became very attached to a rather diminutive Irish pony named Rab, who had a mind of his own. I was taught about saddlery and also learned that if you find, on feeling the girth, that the horse's stomach is blown out, you have to deflate it by giving it a jab with the knee. This I could accept, but not the snaffle bit, which gave long leverage to the curb chain and twisted the curved bit into the roof of the poor animal's mouth, thus tightening the chain on its jaw. That, to my mind, was bordering on cruelty, but it was the accepted practice and I was there to do what I was told.

One outing with Rab still lives with me. The turnout of 'B' Squadron amounted to six horses with which it was necessary to negotiate what was looked on as a busy thoroughfare in those days. Rab was in a frisky mood, ready to go anywhere. On being confronted with a tramcar – no problem – he decided to try to jump over it. It had no business being there. I had quite a shake-up, and with my inexperience of horsemanship, I was lucky to remain in the saddle.

Being taken down by his failed attempt had a soothing effect on Rab, only for his exuberance to surface again at the Riding School when he trod heavily on the hoof of the animal in front. It retaliated in classic Wild West style, lashing out and catching me on the ankle. It was very painful, but to save my face, I gritted my teeth and said nothing.

By now, the nation was holding its breath. Prime Minister Neville Chamberlain's efforts at appeasement, greeted enthusiastically just months before, had done nothing to help. Hitler had gone back on his promises. The Sudetenland had not been saved, and more countries were in imminent danger of being invaded.

With still-clear memories of the Great War, those who had been involved in it must have been most apprehensive, to say the least.

Men & horses of 3 Squadron Scottish Horse, 1939.

Some members of B Troop, Scottish Horse, 1939.

CAVALRY CAPERS

Author and friend at Scottish Horse Camp, 1939.

ONE HORSE POWER

In July 1939, we were off for five days to camp at Blair Atholl in Perthshire, the estate of the Duke of Atholl, founder of the regiment which, from its inception, was his private army, the only one still surviving in Britain today. In the early days, however, no crown appeared on the accoutrement.

When we arrived there, row after row of bell tents met our eyes, and more horses than I had ever seen, a sight to warm the cockles of any man's heart. I pondered over how many men would sleep in each tent – maybe six? Sleeping in a confined space alongside five others would have been a bad enough change for me but, alas, I was somewhat astray in my prediction. There were to be twenty-one, one trooper to each panel of the tent, but the weather was good and I have pleasant memories of my 'Terrier' camp. I was making friends in an entirely fresh environment, and I could let remarks about my ineptitude – for example, 'You should have joined the Camel Corps!' – slide off my back. I knew they were made in fun.

In such company, time passes quickly – someone always has a mouth organ or a Jew's harp. There were sing-songs nearly every night: the old tunes and those played by the big bands on the wireless. We knew all the words, and if we got stuck, we made some up, sometimes in a manner that would have shocked our mothers, but (and you maybe won't believe this but it's perfectly true) alcohol was never even considered. Indeed, it wasn't necessary for us. We were young and care-free, and enjoying this taste of 'work, rest and play' in the companionship of others of the same mind, away from our parents... but still under some supervision of a different kind.

Besides, I was greatly interested in everything we were having to do. I felt quite at home when it came to stripping the Bren gun, a beautiful piece of machinery, as was the Bois rifle, hailed as a terrifying anti-tank weapon. We were assured that, in tests, the carcass of a pig had been penetrated six times by the ricocheting bullet in the interior of a tank. (Not a pleasant thought!) The firing position had been changed from that of the Vickers with toes dug in for recoil, and I can't vouch for the pig, but this rather useless hunk of armoury regularly fractured some part of the human anatomy, usually ankles, at half charge.

The end of our time at Blair Atholl came all too soon, and we returned to normality again, to the daily grind, which wasn't nearly as exciting as what we'd been doing while we were away.

As summer rolled on into autumn, memories of happy days with my father returned, and remembering his death brought many sad moments. I felt sorry for my mother and sister and, somewhat guiltily, I began to wonder if I had acted from a sense of patriotism when I joined the T.A., or if it had been purely escapism. Most of my weekends were now spent with the Terriers, learning about the horrors of war gases, with everlasting lectures. I may suggest that, of all subjects, gas was the most boring, but the implications of being caught out were inconceivable. As Troopers, our weapons were the straight sword and .303 Lee Enfield rifle. Words such as 'windage', 'deflection' and 'trajectory' entered the vocabulary. The firing range at Black Dog near Aberdeen was where we tested our skills … or lack of them.

At work, the completion of an overhead winch, or Telfer car, destined for Woolwich Arsenal, meant that I'd to go there to help erect it on a gantry for the conveyance of artillery pieces. There certainly had been awareness in Scotland of the imminence of war, but in London it appeared as though it had already started. Barrage balloons were floating overhead, most public buildings were surrounded by sandbags, slit trenches were being dug in Hyde Park. The slogan plastered everywhere was, 'Dig for Victory'.

But there couldn't possibly be 'Victory' without some kind of conflict, and war wasn't exactly certain, was it?

I discovered, very shortly, that it was!

On Friday 1 September 1939 I phoned Henderson's in Aberdeen and told them that I was in the Territorial Army and asked permission to return home. I was advised to stay put, but I couldn't help wondering which was more important to me – loyalty to my job or fulfilling the commitment I had made to the Scottish Horse, which would expect all its territorials, whatever their circumstances, to be available whenever they were needed. I made my choice during a sleepless Saturday night, and against orders caught the 6.05 a.m. train from King's Cross the next morning.

At that time, I was too young to appreciate that the work I was doing exempted me from all military service – you can't get much more essential than working in Woolwich Arsenal! But to carry on with my tale, later that same day, while the train was stopped in Perth station, a speech by Mr Chamberlain was relayed over the Tannoy. Because Herr Hitler had ignored the ultimatum he'd been given, Britain was now at war with Germany! I had made the right choice. My country needed me!

It was with mixed feelings that I arrived back in Aberdeen to learn that, during my absence, the Scottish Horse had been mobilised and moved to Dunkeld in Perthshire. It must have been hard for my mother – and indeed, all mothers who had lived through the senseless slaughter of the Great War – to see her son depart so suddenly. It was also difficult for most people to understand why this jumped-up Austrian Corporal had been allowed – only twenty-one short years after the Armistice ending the Great War – to muster sufficient force to trample all over Europe and dictate terms.

On arriving at Dunkeld I was directed to Birnam, only a few miles away, where I was astonished to see that the woods had not moved to Dunsinane, as Shakespeare would have us believe. This was where 'B' Squadron was stationed, and I was shown into a large hall in the Birnam Hotel where army kit was stacked in neat bundles all over the floor. The corporals and sergeants made short work of handing out the items, and by their manner it was easy to see that we weren't playing at soldiers any longer. This was the real thing! You didn't argue, you didn't complain! You couldn't even make a joke to lighten the atmosphere. You took what you were given whether or not you were happy with it.

First impressions had been that sleeping here would be utterly impossible, but with boots correctly arranged for use as a pillow and the illustrious greatcoat – weighing a ton – correctly positioned to do duty as mattress *and* blanket, it wasn't too bad on the floor.

Obviously, I knew and liked most of the lads, we'd trained together for months, and we accepted the excuse, 'There's a war on,' although it did become quite tiresome when it was made to fit all exigencies. The food, prepared in a field kitchen set up alongside the hotel, fell far short of what it should have been, and what good there may have been in it originally had, as often as not, been destroyed in the manner of its cooking. This was before the days of the Army School of Catering, where culinary skills were taught by experts and the meals were on a par with the best of restaurants. In the days I'm describing, a man who didn't know which trade he fancied training for was given the dubious honour of feeding the troopers. Some weren't too bad, of course, but mostly – well, our stomachs just had to grow used to what they gave us.

Although food is never far from the minds of youngsters – because that's really all we were – a sense of seriousness had crept in. Far from 'Hanging Out the Washing on the Siegfried Line', as the great British public were currently singing, we had enough ado to change our socks. Information was beginning to filter through about the rape of Poland, which had been the ultimate trigger for war, and that also unsettled us.

But we didn't have time to brood. Horse lines had to be erected for the expected equine members of our regiment, a long, complicated business. First, a railway sleeper was dug in at an angle and joined to another about 100 yards away by a stout rope. Then, at intervals of ten feet, approximately, two ropes were attached to tether the horse by means of stout straps and shackle pins, which were driven about twelve inches into the ground. Massive deliveries of feeding stuffs arrived – hay and bran mash being the main ingredients. So, what with drills, P.T. and lectures, the days were fairly shortsome, and fully occupied.

Then it came. The Troop Sergeant told us, rather secretively, that the horses would be arriving the following day, and suggested that as it would take at least that day and most of the night to detrain them, I should volunteer for Horse Picket – on duty from 10 p.m. to 6 a.m. – and so have a short night. I did this quite willingly, pleased that I wouldn't be required until the horses were on the line.

London, Midland and Scottish railway (L.M.S.) delivered the goods. Hundreds of horses arrived in the Dunkeld area – those for 'B' Squadron were unloaded near Birnam, the others nearer Dunkeld itself. The orders were to shackle 'fore and aft' … but this wasn't a cowboy picture. This was in dead earnest! We were a nation at war! Moreover, these weren't the hacks we had known, but magnificent ponies, some of them hunters that had competed in the flat and national outings the previous year. The minute I saw them I was lost in admiration of their glossy coats and their streamlined bodies.

But the day was passing and it was dark before our squadron's horses were on the 'lines'. What my superiors had not appreciated, nor could they, was that some of these sensitive animals had previously worked only in pairs, pulling the carriages and coaches of the nobility. Shackling fore and aft proved to be difficult for them. If you have never heard a horse in distress, think yourself lucky! There *are* vicious horses, but, to be honest, very few, and it is generally man who has made them so. In its determination to rejoin its kind, a horse will drive itself to destruction, and by forcing itself to sit down backwards, it can exert a tremendous amount of tension on the shackles.

In the darkness, they are even more difficult to control, and I was one of these first 'pickets'. Stallions reared, as they do, tearing out the fore pins to gain their freedom, and making sure of it by kicking out the rear. The principle of horse lines is that the exertions of a horse on one side will be compensated by similar struggles on the other, but these beasts weren't sticking to the rules. It was even darker by then, and being wartime, there was no chance of getting any lights. Complete blackout! Shambles!

Some of our charges, I suppose, had rebelled in order to join their companions, others in revolt against an environment utterly alien to them. What had we done to these magnificent creatures? Once loose, where could they go? But, absolutely terror-stricken, they set off at a gallop on a headlong rush…to nowhere, with the shackle-pins still attached and lashing at their bellies!

As pickets, of course, we were met with a rather terrifying situation – the thunder of hooves in the absolute blackness. As the night wore on, more horses broke loose, the tension increased, and we discovered the truth of the saying that fear feeds upon itself. Di-dum-di-dum-DI-DUM-DI-DUM! The noise rose to the deafening crescendo of a full stampede. Whether horses have a sonic system, I know not, but to my knowledge, no trooper was hurt that night, in spite of the very real danger of serious injury ever present.

By this time, we were absolutely worn out, but were allowed little or no sleep before orders were given to collect the horses, some from as far away as Perth. This debacle could probably have been regarded as a disgrace, but there was no denying the fact that it had taught us a valuable lesson: *Get to know your horses' backgrounds before trying to discipline them.*

When all this had passed, there was the question of how to allocate the horses. The officers, practically without exception, had their own hunters. They were a race apart, and I believe that most were millionaires or, at the very least, extremely wealthy (the officers, not the horses). I was very pleased with the horse allocated to me. With my trusty steed, my sword and my .303 rifle, I had some power – just one-horsepower, of course, but satisfyingly fulfilling for all that.

A few days later, I was obliged to exchange horses with the sergeant of No.4 Troop – obliged, note, not asked. It appeared that he had chosen a fine animal but had not reckoned on it having such a foul temper. As a Troop Sergeant must be able to move freely amongst the others, it was not doing his image much good when, for no reason, his mount lashed out at something in the passing, so he speedily arranged to swap it for mine. I hadn't had time to form a bond with the steed I had to hand over, but I was still disappointed to see him go. As I've already mentioned, his replacement was a magnificent animal, but his fiery temperament was to get me into some awkward situations. He, too, was given the name 'Rab'.

In the meantime, life was more or less settling down ... into a rigorous routine. Horses have a small stomach, necessitating several feeds per day, the first being at 6 a.m., the last at 10 p.m. Saddlery had to be cleaned and, of course, grooming had to be carried out daily. I still remember the priorities: eyes, nose, ears and dock... the reverse would not have been appreciated. Army horses were well taken care of and, after a long day on exercise, a hot bran mash was eagerly accepted and appreciated to the full.

As the weeks passed, we became hardened to the work, and to the discipline, but there were lighter moments. On the occasion of a regimental parade, after each unit was reported 'all present and correct', the RSM handed his mount over to a trooper and marched off towards the Colonel to report. Unfortunately, the animal had an itch, and in full view of all those assembled, rolled over on its back, a dangerous thing to do when saddled, as the back can be broken. In this instance, however, the horse got up shaking wildly ... with the RSM's sword artistically wrapped around it. Only those who have experienced the wrath of an RSM can fully appreciate what happened then.

On another occasion, the unexpected order to draw swords produced a line of steel blue tips – the unfortunate result of using them to toast bread. Necessity has always been the mother of invention, but I don't think that sergeant appreciated our ingenuity.

Autumn was giving way to winter. Prolonged exercises were taking place – usually in the Tilt (an area of Perthshire) where the ground was pockmarked with deep moorland bogs. Within reason, a horse will pick its own path if left to do so, but will obey the reins if forced. I can picture this incident yet... One of the troopers near me, a cocky sort of individual who thought he knew better than his horse, was determined to make him obey directions. There was a prolonged, personality tussle, but the animal could apparently sense something wrong, or could smell what actually lay ahead. He bucked suddenly, and the trooper, thrown out of the saddle, disappeared into what turned out to be a bog. The stench on him when he came out was absolutely wicked ... as everyone hastened to let him know, to his great humiliation. But I think this episode made him have more respect for his horse.

In those exercises, on the order to charge, swords are drawn, one leans forward along the side of the horse's neck and, with a twist of the arm, it is locked. The excitement and sheer exhilaration is terrific and the bigger the unit, the greater the effect. Hearts pound as quickly as the hooves, adrenaline pumps, horses jostle together and legs are bruised (men's and beasts'). It is the highlight of all cavalry manoeuvres.

Other 'charges' were less inspiring. One event outstanding in my memory was a parade along the Perth road and, owing to occasional traffic, the regiment was in sections of two and must have stretched for several hundred yards. For no reason whatsoever, just sheer equine mischief, Rab decided to have a crafty kick at his companion. Well, that did it! The outraged victim retaliated by lashing out with his hind hooves and planted them in Rab's belly, almost winding him and practically lifting him off the ground.

It was more good luck than good horsemanship that kept me in the saddle as he reared in pain and anger. I have never believed in hard use of the reins, but the slack he got was enough for him to get the bit between his teeth, and he was off. We flashed past 3 Troop of 'B' Squadron, passed 4 Troop of 'A' Squadron and my heart sank when I saw 'HIM' in front.

Rab, however, was no respecter of rank, and we soon overtook the man himself – the Colonel on his white charger!

I'd been 'sawing' Rab's head – this violent pulling on right then left rein was the only way known to me of handling a runaway – but it didn't seem to make much difference. There was quite a high kerb, and Rab decided to gallop with two hooves on one level and two on the other, like a child is wont to do one at a time, but it only confused him, and he came to a gasping halt alongside HQ. It was as if Tonto had lost the Lone Ranger! A horse at full gallop is easy to sit, but it seems to lose all those endearing qualities which made it man's best friend. Thankfully, no action was taken against me for this escapade.

There were difficult times, too. It was the morning feed one day and I had almost filled my lot of hay nets only to find that they were disappearing. I noticed the culprit just on the other side of the line and, as I couldn't lose face, I ran at him with both fists flailing. I knew he was considered to be a bit of a 'hard man' but we had exchanged only a few punches when an officer appeared and our fight was abruptly terminated.

I thought little of it until later that day when I learned that a 'grudge' fight had been set up for us in the local drill hall that night. I didn't feel too happy about this; I could see by the way he handled himself that he knew something about box-ing. A grudge fight is, of course, a fight with no rounds – a fight to a finish. Naturally, everyone turned out to watch, and as I was in 3 Troop and he was in 4, it gave the affair an added boost. Rivalry between the two troops was strong, in a friendly way... most of the time.

Battle commenced and I was soon to receive some stinging blows to the face, which I countered by heavy punches to his body. Raucous yells from the spectators proved that they were thoroughly enjoying this 'feast', which continued for some time. It must have looked as if he were getting the best of it – the face is more vulnerable than the body and I seemed incapable of stopping his lightning jabs – but suddenly there was an almighty scream and my adversary dropped to the floor, writhing in agony.

I was somewhat bewildered but my mates cheered me enthusiastically. The agonised screaming continued, however, and the cheering died away as it dawned on us that this destruction was unlikely to be the result of my blows. It transpired that, in delivering a punch, his thumb had caught, probably against my arm, and had been pushed out of its socket. Nevertheless, despite this being common knowledge, I still enjoyed an enhanced respect for some time afterwards – possibly just because I'd had the guts to stand up and fight such a clearly promising pugilist.

Tent mates.

OF HORSES AND FILLIES

As winter approached, we were bedevilled by lengthy spells of rain and it was turning much colder. Of course, horse blankets were issued, but the churning of hooves had turned the ground to mud and there was no warm air to dry it out. There were days when exercises were impossible and horses had to remain on the 'lines'.

The consequences of this were grim. Mud formed on the fetlocks and drying there brought deep 'cracks' which crippled the animals. This is a very painful condition which is exacerbated by layers of mud continuing to build up. A situation was reached whereby the regiment was losing an average of one horse each and every day. I believe that this was brought to the attention of Parliament, but nothing was done. The reaction had probably been something like – 'What were those stupid Scotsmen complaining about, for goodness sake? Theirs are not the first horses to suffer in war.'

It must have become apparent from the feedback from Europe that this war was not to be won on horseback – however noble the steeds. The Germans were making good use of theirs for transport, but not to my knowledge as cavalry.

During our time together, Rab and I had many good times, but sadly, his days with me were numbered. The whole question of the use of horses in this role had apparently been debated upon and revised. It had also become politically sensitive as more notice was being taken of it by the newspapers. It was almost with relief, therefore, that I watched him being loaded into a horse-box to be taken to ... destination unknown. Then, on 31 December 1939, the whole regiment was moved out of Perthshire – bound for England.

Our destination was the estate of the Duke and Duchess of Portland at Welbeck, near Worksop. The horses for other ranks had disappeared, but along with the officers, many of the senior NCOs retained their mounts. I did miss Rab, but this was a new experience for me – in brief, I became batman to Sergeant Major Davies, a PSI (Permanent Staff Instructor) from the Scots Greys. Although a disciplinarian, he had a human side and, what was more important to me, HE HAD A HORSE!

Having approved of what we saw as we were transported through the grounds, our accommodation, unfortunately, came as a bit of a shock. Our home was what had originally been perfectly adequate stables, but where one horse had previously bedded down, six of us were expected to manage. In fairness, though, after a week or so, better billets were provided in a larger area. The beds were arranged as in a hospital ward, except that they were much closer together, but still much preferable to what we'd been given at first.

In the meantime, the fear and likelihood of invasion was becoming ever more real. Dawn and dusk patrols were organised, each man being issued with five rounds of .303 ammunition to deal with any bogus 'paratroopers' we might chance upon. This was a very real threat, but fortunately for us, none crossed our path. I did, however, have one slightly bizarre and quite far-reaching encounter.

On my way back to billets one night, a middle-aged chap driving a lovely Bentley stopped and offered me a lift, which I gratefully accepted. Petrol being severely rationed by this time, it did cross my mind to wonder how he managed to keep this powerful car on the road. It was no secret that petrol could be obtained if one had the right contacts, or knew how to go about it – farmers, for instance, had an allowance for starting up tractors which, once started, ran on paraffin – so I wasn't exactly suspicious of him, but it was best to be careful. He didn't ask one single question that was in the least out of place, and it turned out that I was to see much more of him in the near future. In fact, he was to introduce me to a girl who would come to mean quite a lot to me.

Horses were meantime exercised in the maze of underground tunnels – big enough to accommodate a heavy goods vehicle let alone a horse – which spread through the estate, and being the property of a premier duke, Welbeck was superior to most of its kind. On seeing the mansion for the first time, it seemed to me to have a room for every day of the year, though 365 may have been a slight exaggeration. I can say in all honesty, however, that the church also within the grounds was absolutely magnificent. .

My Bentley acquaintance turned out to be a doctor of medicine and was clearly well-to-do, but for some reason, probably because he didn't *have* to earn his living, he chose not to practise. We became very friendly and he took me to dine occasionally at some of the most exclusive hotels in Sheffield, where, even when the dining rooms were full, we were given prompt attention – no standing around waiting. This was privilege! Money was not a problem, and occasional late passes were issued despite being rationed.

I can't explain why this man paid me so much attention (nothing out of place). It was as if he thought he owed a debt to the soldiers stationed at Welbeck, especially Scotsmen, and who was I to refuse? I'd never been one to question a gift horse. I must admit that I felt a little out of my depth at first – for instance, I'd never heard of the humble tattie being called a *pomme-de-terre* before – but it wasn't long until I was behaving as if I'd been born with a silver spoon in my mouth and was well accustomed to this kind of life.

It was during one of these outings that he made the introduction I mentioned earlier, to a really attractive young lady known as 'Chip', with whom I got on very well right from the start. During the course of that evening, she told me there was to be a dinner dance at Lord Sandbeck's residence, and suggested that I should escort her to it. This, naturally, raised two problems for me: first, I didn't have anything suitable to wear, and second, and even more difficult, I'd no chance of getting a late pass. The whole British Army was supposed to be confined to barracks at the time because invasion by the enemy, which had been lurking in the background for some time, was almost certain now.

The first problem was overcome in a most unexpected fashion. I was taken to a tailor and measured for a Scottish Horse dress uniform, complete with boots and spurs. These uniforms were quite spectacular in navy blue with a yellow leg stripe and chain mail on the shoulders, and I looked forward to being properly dressed for once. More to the point, I wasn't even expected to pay for this rig-out!

How to get there, however? This, too, was settled when the lady I was to accompany arrived discreetly near the gates where, wearing my greatcoat over my finery, I speedily joined her. And the late pass? Knowing it would have been pointless, I hadn't asked, but with great presence of mind, I'd made up a dummy bed and could only hope for the best.

On arrival at the dance, I entered another new world… wine, women and song, far removed from the small floor at Birnam. Officers of all ranks were there, some above colonel, and I was particularly interested in the army chaps with red epaulettes, in other words, those of Field Rank. But they, like everyone else, were intent on enjoying themselves and paid no heed to me.

The time passed most enjoyably. Chip and I were perfect dancing partners, but while we were sitting regaining our breath after one particularly boisterous Paul Jones, she looked earnestly at me and murmured, 'I feel a little privacy is called for, don't you?'

Scarcely able to credit what she seemed to be suggesting, my heartbeats accelerated to a kind of military two-step, but I managed a nonchalant smile. 'Will we go and see if we can find somewhere to be alone?' (My friends in Aberdeen would have been amazed at my refined accent... I think.)

We set off to look, only to discover that others had had the same idea before us. On gingerly opening doors, we were confronted by many illuminating spectacles, the first an expanse of bare thigh, which made my pulse lose all sense of rhythm and pound as fast as it could. Most of the rest we glimpsed had got well beyond that stage. Unsuccessful in our quest for even a small corner to ourselves, we decided to make the most of it in the car. All good things should not be reserved for the favoured few.

On occasion, when I applied for a late pass, I got one, on others, I didn't. I knew that if my Troop Sergeant suddenly made up his mind to be difficult, this nonsense would have to come to an abrupt end. As it was, the high life was catching up on me. One morning after a late night, followed by having to be on parade for early patrol, sleep got the better of me and on seeing a Bren ammunition box close at hand, I stretched out and used it as a pillow. Oh yes, it was dark... at first! Thank goodness a friendly boot roused me before someone in authority became aware of this slumbering soldier.

In the meantime, events in Europe were moving nearer to disaster. The Low Countries had been overrun and it was quite obvious that France would follow. There was little hope of British servicemen of any kind hanging out washing on the

Siegfried Line – at least not in the foreseeable future – and as it turned out, not for some years. This period was known as the 'phoney war', yet an ominous foreboding pervaded throughout. It looked as though the German war machine would not stop at the Channel. The fall of France, resulting in the miraculous evacuation at Dunkirk, is history, of course, and has been described by so many men better qualified than I to do so that I shall leave it at that.

Patrols were stepped up and the atmosphere was tense – but moves were afoot which were to bring about vast changes to me and to hundreds of others. In no time at all, the Scottish Horse was disbanded altogether – utter sacrilege – and divided into the 79th and 80th Regiments Royal Artillery, and so ended my sojourn at Welbeck.

I might mention here that although I never saw the doctor again, I did see Chip…

Chip

ARTILLERY ANTICS

Our next destination was Grimsby, and conversion to artillery in the shape of six-inch howitzers had us now named the 79th Medium Regiment R.A. The six-inch howitzer was a clumsy piece of machinery firing a 100-lb shell, and it did little to boost the morale to see the words 'For drill purposes only' marked along the 'piece'.

Our purpose was the coverage of the Humber estuary and, in particular, Immingham Docks, although Adolf would have burst his sides laughing with one glance at our line of defence. Once the gun was in position, the first job was to dig a slit trench nearby, then a rope was attached to the firing mechanism and back into the trench, in case the howitzer blew itself up, which was a very real danger. One jerk on this rope brought an almighty roar as the monster discharged its deadly cargo.

I was intrigued by the whole procedure, which was really quite simple – the Regiment was to lay down a predicted shoot into a designated area or target. This strategy appeared to pay off, because almost every night at 10 p.m. we were visited by the Luftwaffe, and although our gun positions were never hit, the Hun was obviously giving the area a high priority ... but they were aiming for the Docks, naturally, not our antiques.

We were in the era of the Fifth Column, walls having ears, posters advising us to 'Be Like Dad and Keep Mum!' and rumours abounding galore. It's strange, isn't it, how otherwise normal persons can get carried away when passing on a titbit they've heard, always adding an extra part to a story in order to make it more interesting... or more unbelievable. A rigorous blackout was obviously essential, and anyone flouting it ran the risk of being at the receiving end of a .303 bullet. A high degree of discipline involving ceaseless practice was maintained.

The details of gunnery are involved, so I'll just try to give a superficial understanding. An area or target is given a priority which dictates the firepower and type of weapons. Topography has to be considered; it's no good using a high velocity flat trajectory missile if obstructions exist in its intended path. It is in these circumstances that the howitzer comes into its own and is invaluable. The projectile is rammed into the breach and a charge No.1-4 is inserted, depending on the range and required elevation of the 'piece'.

Plots are now charted, fixing the gun position and that of its target by means of co-ordinators (map references). Guns are then aligned by turning the slipping scale of the sight in accordance with the director reading (this is a type of theodolite). These guns being rather clumsy, it is desirable that all targets be within the traverse of the gun, as the spade (end of the gun) movement is slow and cumbersome. Targets should therefore be within these capacities.

As you have no doubt gathered, I was fascinated by all this, and my obvious interest brought me the rank of Lance Bombardier and the designation GPOA (Gun Position Officer's Assistant) in my opinion, a pretty impressive handle to bear.

There are three Artillery shoots:-

    1.   Visual target
    2.   Ranging to target by bracketing
    3.   Predicted shoot

The first is unusual, as these guns should not be so positioned; after all, the enemy is sometimes outrageous enough to fire back. The other two are more common, demanding observation by either manned posts or from the air.

Our stay there did involve a predicted shoot, when all guns were laid on specific sea areas and could hit them in any weather or light. Not so a Battery of 25-pounders ahead of us, however. A ranging shell of theirs, on its flat trajectory, passed right through a house, luckily without fatality. I will leave it at that, because – as in all such cases – there were many variations of what went wrong. The rumour-mongers had a field day… several days, in fact.

The course of the war looked even more disastrous now. There seemed to be nothing to stop the *blitzkrieg*, and it was frustrating not to be able to do something about it, to feel so utterly helpless. The Battery, however, was then directed to Shepshed, a small town near Loughborough, where further training was done. I have little recollection of this period – nothing much out of the ordinary could have taken place – apart from one engagement which caused me some alarm.

On being questioned regarding my boxing ability, I hastened to explain that my victory at Birnam – news of which had apparently followed me – had been sheer luck.

The sergeant frowned. 'Bloody hard luck, then. I've put you down to fight a sergeant from the Scots Guards in the Town Hall at Loughborough, so don't you f***ing let me down. They're cocky buggers as it is, them Guards.'

I had to bow to fate. My life would be made absolute hell if I defaulted, but as the time for the match loomed menacingly ever nearer, maybe I did consider reporting sick. The only thing stopping me was awareness that the MO would know I was swinging the lead, and wouldn't play along with it. I wasn't a coward, not really, but it was awful to carry on as usual when common sense was telling me I'd be pounded to a pulp in just a few days, but what else could I do? I'd be a laughing stock if I refused.

My mental suffering at that time was very great, agonising over which would inflict most injuries on me, a defeat at the hands of a Scots Guardsman, or a going-over from my own mob because I'd let them down. But someone up there must have been looking after me! My prayers were answered! The Regiment was actually moved out before the fixture took place. Not a lie, I swear!

I was one of four motor-cyclists who headed north with the transporters. Bad weather had set in and the roads were extremely treacherous. By mischance, I had quite a spectacular crash while overtaking the convoy, hitting ice and being catapulted over the handlebars. My guardian angel must still have been in attendance, thank goodness, and it was my 'tin' hat that took the initial impact, but even though my face was badly torn, all I could do was get back on the Norton and catch up with my comrades. After almost sixty years, I still have some of the marks to remind me of that mishap.

As we moved farther and farther north, the weather grew progressively worse until it was verging on the impossible, so it was with great relief that we received instructions that all motor cycles were to be loaded into trucks. The final part of our journey was only slightly more comfortable, certainly less risky, but probably not so invigorating. I was astonished when our destination turned out to be the village of Insch, some 30 miles north of Aberdeen... my home town.

I'll never forget our billets there – three of us in a council house bedroom with only one bed – talk about sardines! – and we were all big lads. By this time the winter of 1941 had set in with a vengeance and the aluminium hot water bottle in our bed was more than welcome... but not when held against an unprotected part of the body by a mischievous bedmate, which happened fairly often, youths being youths even then.

But we'd never been in accommodation as cramped as this before, and we wondered dolefully how long we'd have to put up with it. You can imagine, therefore, how our spirits were raised when we heard rumours that Insch was simply a staging post for Huntly, just a matter of 15 miles farther on. Without doubt we would get better billets there. We surely couldn't get any worse!

The conduct of the war, the weather and the food shortages all accounted for a somewhat more serious attitude. The fact that a train supposedly carrying Prince Bernhard of the Netherlands had got stuck in a snowdrift quite near where we were did not fill us with an overpowering urge to go to his aid, because the 'rescue' had to be carried out in atrocious conditions. Not one man, however, reported sick, and the train, bearing the Prince or not, was released from its confines.

Once again, the earlier rumours proved to be true. A massive build-up of the 51ˢᵗ Highland Division was being effected in the Huntly area, and our move there was soon accomplished. A number of Nissen huts had been erected near the main road on the outskirts of the town, and a local church hall served as a mess, but for whatever the reason, the food was grim – not more than one slice of bread at any meal, and a fork aimed at a sardine brought a splatter of guts on to the plate.

Another, newer, element contributed to the general dissatisfaction. The call-up had now been extended to include older men, and being accustomed to all the home comforts a wife can provide, they didn't take kindly to army life. They were inclined to moan about things, and, naturally enough, their thoughts were mostly of their families. It was entirely different for us as bachelors. We'd been Terriers, volunteers, so we had no one but ourselves to blame if things weren't quite what we'd imagined. Plus, we were young, out for adventure… and for fun, when, where and if we could get it. Still, listening to a steady stream of complaints did get us down.

It would be roughly around this time that I heard of the possibility of suitable army personnel being allowed to transfer to the RAF to take on aircrew duties. In spite of wondering if there was some sort of catch to it, I rushed to put my name down as soon as it became official. If I was accepted, I told myself jubilantly, I'd be happy with whatever duties I was given, no matter how demeaning or repugnant to me, as long as they took me in contact with even one aeroplane. With that in mind, I was prepared to wait for as long as it took those in authority to make their selection.

Manoeuvres in the Cabrach and surrounding area with live ammunition were carried out, but on these exercises it seemed beyond the wit of whoever was responsible to feed us or to let us feed ourselves. On one occasion, we had moved into our third gun position before we were given time out to eat, but on our eager approach to the field kitchen, we were sadly disillusioned. I can still clearly picture the perfect rainbow-like arc of paraffin from a pressurised cooker being mirrored in the sunshine as it fell back on all that was eatable… thus rendering it uneatable!

These manoeuvres were being adjudged by a very senior officer who emphasised, in no uncertain terms at a subsequent conference, that if the men could not be properly fed, he would have to insist on the giving up of one of the guns. As this was considered the greatest disgrace in the Royal Artillery, the threat was enough, and did much to improve our circumstances.

Some weeks later, I was delighted on being told that an interview had been arranged for me at RAF HQ, Edinburgh, and on attending, I was shown into an office where sat an awe-inspiring Group Captain with a black patch over one eye. It wasn't only the medals on his chest that gained my instant respect, but also his commanding demeanour... and what was more, he had his 'wings'. *Hell's Angels* came flooding back to me, and when it struck me that my boyhood dream of being a pilot perhaps stood a chance of being realised – something I had never truly believed possible – I vowed that I would do my best to make it so. Perhaps I'd never actually be a pilot, but just to be in an aircraft in whatever capacity would do me.

The interview was quite searching, including the classic, 'Why do you want to join the Air Force?'

I remember replying to the effect that I thought it essential that Hitler be stopped, and that I felt I could contribute something as aircrew, the usual platitudes most applicants would trot out. The difference was that I really meant them.

'It's not as glamorous as you imagine,' I was told bluntly. 'You will be in close contact with the enemy, and survival is not guaranteed.'

If this warning was intended to dim my aspirations of getting into the air, it failed dismally. I was next shown into what might be called an 'angle room' where the location of a variety of objects was related to a control system apparently devised to determine what was at an angle and what appeared to be level. I was told that the instruments were accurate, and must be obeyed, and I followed the instructions to the letter.

Numerous other tests followed, including round pins in square holes, etc., then I was given a thorough medical examination, at the end of which, apart from a remark about my teeth, I appeared to satisfy requirements as far as fitness was concerned.

I didn't see the Group Captain again, but I would have been interested to know more about him – how he lost his eye, for one thing. I left feeling somewhat dazed and caught a train back to Huntly. I had at least attempted to fulfil my ambition to fly, but in what capacity, if at all, was for the future to reveal...

I hadn't lost respect for the Regiment, now the 79th Med. Regiment RA. I had tried to follow a dream and volunteered to be part of what was a very different animal.

One day quite soon after I'd been for the all-important interview, the Orderly Officer visited the mess and asked, as was the practice, 'Any complaints?'

I don't know if it was the hope that I might not be there for much longer, but I found myself saying, in a rather audacious manner, 'Well, as a matter of fact, some of the meals are ... to put it plainly ... uneatable.'

I should have anticipated his reply, given with pinched mouth, flared nostrils and glittering eyes: 'There's a war on, Corporal!'

I should have been grateful that it was no worse than that, but I was already wondering if I'd spoiled my chances of rising to the top. And would a bad report precede me if I was accepted for the RAF and ruin my chances there, too? I didn't regret what I'd done, though, however pointless it turned out. At least I'd tried.

What was so maddening was the fact that good rations *were* being supplied, even with a war on, but some went missing, some were diluted and some were simply stolen. After all these years, I still get upset about this. Those responsible were cheating on their own mates, and I wish I had taken the matter further at the time.

The result of my medical in Edinburgh wasn't long in being forwarded. At the Battery Office, I was handed a slip which read only, 'Requires fillings prior to transfer.' I was overjoyed that the RAF was still interested in me, but the thought of the dentist…? Not a coward?

It transpired that I would be one of a party going to Keith (only about 10 miles away) to have our teeth brought up to standard. It was a memorable experience, each of us trying to prove that he didn't give a fig about dentists, the jokes and ditties bandied about were getting bluer and bluer, until we reached our destination. The dental centre was a disused shop, and about six of us were seated on a long bench at what would have been the customer's side of the counter. In time, a dentist appeared almost brandishing a large syringe… and striking us dumb with terror. As he consulted what may have been medical records, he went blithely along the line, putting lethal injections into our gums – and using the same needle throughout!

I have little recollection of what happened to me then, as centre stage was taken by one poor devil who had come to have some extractions. The deed done, he moved around spitting blood and soon strayed into the area behind the counter. Little did he know that a trapdoor on the floor there had inadvertently been left open. *Shades of Sweeney Todd!* He disappeared with an agonised yell and sustained further injuries. The homeward journey was much quieter than the outward, I can assure you.

I will admit that, in all our time at Huntly, we never really got our act together. Map reading was atrocious; our guns were relics from the Great War and many were finding it difficult to accept life with the military. This was the atmosphere that pervaded during my last weeks in the army.

I must point out, however, that even without me – or possibly because of being without me – the Regiment went on to perform sterling services and distinguished itself later in the war when re-equipped with 5.5-inch guns.

When the time came for me to leave the Artillery, it was bad enough saying goodbye to my comrades, some I'd been with for years, but I found it just as emotional to go to the Quarter Master and hand in my equipment. It was as if I could still see, through misted eyes, my friend Rab – my one horse power!

Colleagues with field gun.

Sergeant Jameson's Gun

Author (far left) with colleagues from the Scottish Horse.

With Scottie at Shepshed.

THE RAF ~ A DREAM COME TRUE

RAF training.

CADETSHIP

My posting was to St. John's Wood, London and I was now an RAF cadet. Only those with Regular Army rank were allowed to retain it, so I had lost my stripe, but the white flash on my air force blue forage cap more than compensated. This was an entirely different kettle of fish. Just being a part, however humble, of this youngest branch of the services was thrill enough for me, and sleeping between sheets and having good food was a bonus. All drills were arduous and marching was done at 130 steps per minute, but I must have done reasonably well, because I was then posted to Initial Training Wing at Newquay, Cornwall and billeted at the Beaconsfield Hotel.

The going was tough – physically and mentally! Hanging from the roofs of our classrooms were 70 models of allied and enemy aircraft. We were bluntly told that by the end of our six-week stay we would be expected to correctly identify each and every one of them, not only by its full shape, but by seeing even a small part of it; also we should know the field of the fire of its guns.

The need for this knowledge became blatantly obvious and more or less dictated the style of attack which should be adopted. A number of enemy aircraft were caught out and destroyed by the fitting of a gun turret behind the pilot in a Boulton Paul Defiant single-engined machine, before the Luftwaffe realised that it should not be attacked from the rear, where all other fighters were vulnerable.

Physical fitness was every bit as important as our education, and became more and more demanding. The Beaconsfield Hotel was on the seafront and unless we could convince the Physical Training Instructor that it was impossible, we had to swim from the beach into the harbour – no mean feat! To turn back was 'a poor show' and the only alternative was a cross-country run.

At the end of this course we were granted fourteen days leave and this is where I took it into my head to be a naughty boy and take a 'wee detour' before going home to see my mother. Although it took me twelve hours, my journey from Newquay to London was made in comparative comfort because I had the luxury of actually getting a seat. At King's Cross, I found a phone box and contacted Chip, my friend in Doncaster – the young lady I'd been introduced to by the doctor in Welbeck, if you remember – and arranged to stop off there to see her. On asking one of the railwaymen, I was assured that my train did indeed stop at Doncaster... but alas it didn't! It went right through to York.

Determined not to give up, I caught a southbound train... which also flashed past my intended destination. I got off at Grantham, about as far south of Doncaster as York was north, and conditions as a result of overcrowding were bad. Not my day! I'd had enough of trains by this time and took to the road to get a lift. Luckily, I didn't have long to wait until a large truck drew up and I clambered aboard. First telling the driver how grateful I was to him for stopping, I explained about my unplanned and unwelcome travels.

He gave me a searching glance. 'Have you ever handled anything like this?' he asked, sounding wearily hopeful.

'No,' I said, quite truthfully.

'There's nothing to it, mate.'

Estimating that his speed could hardly be exceeding 20 mph I was very tempted to have a go and casually asked, 'What kind of load are you carrying?'

He shrugged, then before I could press him for an answer, he mumbled, 'Explosives.'

His eyes met mine ruefully, and we both thought better of his suggestion. I could understand why he'd made it, though. He was clearly thoroughly exhausted, possibly having gone without sleep for some considerable time. It was with great relief, therefore, that I reached Doncaster all in one piece and met up with Chip, whom I hadn't seen since I left Welbeck.

As a well-brought-up young lady, her first question after a lingering, very affectionate, greeting, was, 'When was the last time you had anything to eat?'

'I've had nothing since early this morning,' I had to admit.

She took me to a pricey hotel restaurant, clearly her sort of place, and even though I wasn't in the habit of wolfing down my food, I made short work of what she ordered for me. I was so pleased to be in her company again that I hardly noticed what I ate. This was also why I can't remember where she took me afterwards – I do have a faint recollection of it being a concert of some sort which had been laid on for the troops, but whether it was an orchestra giving a rendition of some classical pieces, one of the big bands playing popular songs, or one of the ENSA shows, I wouldn't like to say. Whatever, I was ecstatically happy to be sitting so close to her, arm along the back of her chair, legs touching.

Then, as a finale to a wonderful evening, came what I'd been hoping for. She drove to a country lane where we settled into the back of the car, and it wasn't until the wee sma' hours that she dropped me off at the station and we said a clinging 'Goodbye'.

With some time to wait for a train to Aberdeen, I settled back on one of the wooden benches and dozed off for a couple of hours. It was approximately 4 a.m., when I made the devastating discovery – I'd lost my ticket! When my heart started beating again, I decided that this was just another in the long line of mishaps, hitches, whatever you like to call those things often sent to try us, and I'd manage to overcome it. I made my way along the platform, located the RTO's office and told the only occupant my predicament. Could he possibly help me?

I was about half-way through the necessary form filling when the next blow came.

'You'll have to pay for another ticket, mate,' the clerk said, raising his head for a moment. His eyes held a curious mixture of emotions – censure (at me for being so careless), annoyance (that he was being called on to do all this extra paperwork) and more than a touch of sympathy. Only his bald statement made any impact on me.

'Oh no!' I was flabbergasted, and not particularly cheered when he said that it would come off my credits, because my credits at that time were not exactly what anyone would call buoyant.

'I'd better look for the one I lost,' I told the somewhat bewildered man, although I didn't hold out much hope of finding it.

I ran out of the station, retracing the journey Chip and I had made in the car. My mind on other things, I hadn't taken much notice of the route, yet I was quite sure that the most likely spot I could have lost this very important piece of paper was the lane where we had parked. The call of nature had taken me out of the car at one point, so it could have fallen out of the pocket of my tunic then. It was my only hope! If I'd dropped it anywhere else, even inside the car, I may as well forget it.

It was coming up to 5 o'clock. I judged that I'd between two and three miles to go, and the Aberdeen train was due to leave Doncaster shortly after six. Panic! You know the feeling? That no matter what you do or where you look, you're not going to find whatever it is you're looking for? And even if you do, it'll likely be too late.

I was growing ever more breathless with running, a stitch had started in my side, and I doubted if I'd a chance in hell of making it, when I saw a police sergeant standing at a street corner... holding a bicycle. It was one of those rare moments when, at your wits' end to know what to do, something crops up and gives birth to a flash of inspiration in your befuddled brain. He wasn't aware of it, but this man could be my saviour. Not wanting to make any kind of slip, I approached him carefully.

He smiled, glad of someone to speak to. 'You look a bit lost, lad. Can I help?'

There was no time for niceties, so I launched straight into it. After giving him a very brief outline of my predicament, I asked, pleaded, 'Would you save my life and give me a loan of your bike? Please?' (If you think this was an outrageous thing to do, remember that it was wartime, when people did things they would never have dreamt of doing at any other time.)

I almost passed out with despair in the couple of seconds it took him to think it over, and I wondered if my request was stretching the realms of early-morning-acquaintance a bit too far, or undermining police relations with the public. I therefore offered him my watch as collateral, and hastily added my almost full packet of Senior Service (I'm sure this last was what swung the balance in my favour; civilians could hardly get cigarettes for love nor money at the time) ... and he handed over the bicycle. This whole episode may sound un-believable, but I swear every word of it is perfectly true.

To stretch the realms of credibility even further, I did find what I was looking for, although I've often wondered about this. The chances of finding a lane I'd only been in once were absolutely minimal, never mind coming across such a small item as a train ticket. Anyway, I pedalled hell-for-leather back to the police sergeant, who heaved a sigh of relief when I hove in sight. I bet he thought he'd never see me again – nor his bike.

'You got it, then?' he asked, a bit unnecessarily, I thought, for my grin must have told him. Pulling my watch and the Senior Service out of his pocket, he held them out to me, so I took the watch – being a present from my mother it had sentimental value – but as I strapped it on, I noticed how wistfully he looked at the packet still in his hand.

Big-hearted, I smiled, 'Keep the fags as a thank-you for the loan of the bike.' It was a gesture made on the spur of the moment, but the gratitude in his eyes made up for having to go without cigs till I got home.

'Will you manage to make your train,' he asked, stuffing his prize back in his pocket.

'I damn-well hope so!'

I took to my heels, sprinting as I'd never sprinted before, and eventually caught the train to Aberdeen… by the skin of my teeth.

I must have slept for the first two days, but it was good to be back in the bosom of my family. In comparison with cities in England, I suppose my home town got off fairly lightly. Despite being the most frequently bombed city in Scotland, Aberdeen had not come off worst, although some fairly heavy raids *had* caused a considerable loss of life in several areas.

Having caught up on my lost sleep, I met up with Alfie McDonald, a pal from the Terriers, and we were walking across Union Bridge, high above the railway line (where I had stood as a boy to watch the trains puffing out of from underneath the arches on their way to Inverness), when there was a violent explosion that seemed to come from the direction of the Joint Station. There had been no air raid warning, not that we'd heard, anyway, but a piece of shrapnel landed on the street a little ahead of us. Alfie ran to pick up what would be a souvenir worth keeping, but dropped it with a screech to inspect the nasty burn it had left on the palm of his hand. To this day, I have never unravelled that incident. If it *had* been a bomb, there was no report of it in the newspapers, not even the locals, but Alfie's hand was definitely burned and extremely painful. I can't explain it. One of life's eternal mysteries, I suppose, like the *Marie Celeste*, but not so well known. Not known at all, really, except by Alfie and me.

Everything was going smoothly at home, but it hurt me to see the change in my mother. She clearly hadn't got over my father's death even yet, and was finding her sorrow hard to bear. She had lived through the slaughter of the Great War and, as the Group Captain had said at my interview in Edinburgh, my survival was not guaranteed – no more than anyone else's – which, although I hadn't told her, she must have realised for herself. Losses of aircrew were already heavy, and I shouldn't even have been in the services. Hadn't I been exempt from military service in the first place, owing to my reserved occupation?

Mother had aged while I was away. Caught off-guard, she looked down-hearted, dejected, although having me home for a short time did go a little way to cheer her. Or was that just a face she put on for me? But I was still young enough to crave excitement, adventure, and I'm afraid that I spent more time wandering round town than sitting at home with her.

During this leave, I saw the fortifications at the beaches; a rocket battery had been located on the Queen's Links and the pillboxes were manned. I heard accounts of German raids, and great was local pride in the Spitfires from Dyce Aerodrome which had engaged and shot down a lone bomber one lunch-time. It had caused a tremendous amount of mayhem in the city, making a direct hit on one of the ship-building yards and killing quite a few men on their lunch break, also wreaking havoc on some residential areas, with substantial fatalities and demolition of homes.

It had been thought that the Heinkel would crash on a housing estate near the Bridge of Dee but, fortunately, it landed on the partly built ice-rink nearby, thus saving many lives. Whether this was a result of the German pilot's expertise in his last few minutes of life, or of Divine intervention, no one will ever know. One thing only is certain: the ice rink was never built, and where a wrecked enemy bomber once lay, there now stands another, not particularly attractive or inspiring, housing estate.

I later met a Czechoslovakian pilot who had been involved in this incident, who made a quaint remark – 'Spitfire like lady... beautiful machine.'

My world was in two compartments at this time. On the one hand, my family and the places I had known as a boy, and on the other, training to identify the blind spots in German aircraft and their inferiority in manoeuvrability, which skill was to save my life on more than one occasion in the future.

I enjoyed my leave, but I couldn't hide my delight, and pride, when papers arrived telling me to report to EFTS (Elementary Flying Training School). I'd been accepted for training as a pilot at Cambridge!

Oh, happy, happy day! It was not *Hell's Angels* by any stretch of the imagination, but it was a foot on the bottom step!

FLYING TRAINING

My time at EFTS was more or less divided between lectures and flying, and, of course, the excitement was terrific. I think my account would probably make more sense if I mentioned some of the subjects we had to tackle:-

1. Theory of flight
2. Air Navigation
3. Ballistics.

1) Flight, I learned, is brought about by the contours of an airfoil. The propeller (airscrew) is itself an airfoil, thus dragging the aircraft forward. This sounds ponderous for what looks like effortless movement in the air, but there's no arguing – it works!

2) Navigation is, naturally, based on compass bearings, which are only applicable in still air. We've now got a triangle of forces bringing about the difference between the track and heading of the machine. In slower aircraft, this deviation is considerable, and I had to learn it the hard way.

3) Ballistics deals with all the forces acting on a projectile and the ability to strike a moving object. I found these lectures intensely interesting, and my knowledge of mathematics helped me immensely. I was also blessed with a feeling for engines...and the love I'd had for them right from boyhood, as I've already explained.

The great day came! I was kitted out with flying equipment, and my instructor was F/O McCann, an Aussie of fighting experience. The movements of the control surfaces were pointed out, and it was emphasised that I must forever be aware of their proper function. I was strapped into a pilot parachute and told to get into the front seat of a Tiger Moth.

I won't bore you with all the drill, although it *must* be followed. Suffice to say, the fitter pulled the inverted Gypsy engine over top dead centre, and after 'switches on' and 'contact', it purred into life. 'Chocks away' and we were off. I was surprised at the response of the aircraft, especially the effect of a blip on the throttle – the slightest touch made a big difference. I was ecstatic! I was flying! I was actually FLYING!

It was, of course, the start of 'circuits and bumps' (explained later). Amongst other things, I learned that it was cold up there in this open-cockpit machine and McCann seemed to have more confidence in me than I had. I'd to force myself to remember that this was not an air circus but the prelims to war in the air, yet as turns developed into steep turns and the ability to complete a roll of some kind, I became besotted with aerobatics. I couldn't get enough of it. This is what I'd visualised when, as a young boy, I lay in bed after seeing *Hell's Angels.* This is what I was meant for.

At last, the longed-for, if a little apprehensively, time arrived. We landed as usual and McCann jumped out. 'Carry on!' he said, grinning like the Cheshire cat.

My first solo ... alone ... on my own ... by myself ... how many other ways can I say it? Up there in the clouds!

Heart pounding. Taxi out. Take off. Gain height... It was an experience like no other I'd ever had, nerve-shatteringly, breathtakingly, pride-fully exhilarating. I think I made a reasonable landing for a first attempt. At any rate, I walked away from it – on legs that had some difficulty in performing properly. I only wished that my father had been there to see this achievement. But maybe he was. Of course he was! Watching his son displaying his aeronautical prowess.

The date was 12 October 1941.

Air navigation from Cambridge is aided by Ely Cathedral... at least, it was for me; I don't know about the other pilots. The test came when I was told to fly to Booker Airfield, London. I reached my destination with no problems, got the necessary signature to confirm that I'd been there and was also given the wind-speed I had to allow for on my return journey. Unfortunately, I was to find that this last wasn't entirely accurate, which, as you can guess, played merry hell with my calculations, a tricky situation. It's easy to imagine that what you see on the ground is what's on the map, making it easy to pinpoint your position, but not so. I got lost! Admitting this to myself, I looked for a place to land. I soon spotted a field, quite a small field but it looked inviting and I'd surely have room to set the aircraft down there. I can proudly and, more to the point, truthfully say that I did – with a few yards to spare.

Only minutes later, I was amazed to see a lovely girl coming towards me, so lovely that, to use a well-worn cliché, I wondered if I'd crashed and was in a place not of this world, but this angel turned out to be a perfectly normal human being. She insisted on taking me to her home, where I met her family.

I tried to tell them I was just a cadet on initial training, but they treated me as though I'd won the Battle of Britain – entirely single-handed. In fact, I was still in the Scottish Horse at the time that particular battle was raging, but I didn't disillusion them. I'd discovered that it was quite nice being a hero.

Humiliation came after the airfield had been contacted! McCann arrived, and he was, to put it mildly, rather unforgiving! I said a humbled goodbye to my hosts.

It's not easy to take off from a small area with two on board where only one had landed, despite experience. A savage burst on the throttle got us airborne, which took a great weight off my mind. No damage had been done!

It was later confirmed that I'd been given a wrong wind speed at Booker. I was not to blame for the mishap. PHEW!

In those years, it was unnatural to live devoid of congenial company. Doncaster was not all that far away, Chip was a very attractive girl and, better still, she had a Hillman 10, so we managed to see each other occasionally and get around... within limits. It was during those times that I revisited Welbeck and actually went round several of the spots I'd come to know while I was exercising the Sergeant Major's horse. My relationship with Chip was, um, very friendly, and we thoroughly enjoyed each other's company.

Sadly, leisure was strictly rationed and, what with night flying and studies, the days were never long enough. I did manage to complete 116 flying hours, however, and was given an 'Above Average' assessment. I therefore left No.22 EFTS and transferred to No.17 EFTS at Peterborough.

Here I was given instruction on the Link Trainer – a weird machine, but invaluable for instrument flying. It had a fully equipped cockpit over which a canopy excluded all light. It took me back to Edinburgh and the ability to rely purely on instruments except in a stall, which is when the gyro topples and renders instruments useless. This, you will understand, is quite dangerous in cloud or at low level.

It wasn't all serious, thankfully, there were lighter moments, such as landing on fields to collect mushrooms. No, I am definitely not kidding, though I could hardly believe it myself.

We'd been circling round quite a large field when my instructor gave the whimsical order, 'Put her down there, Jock.' (Jock? When I'm practically a fully-fledged pilot? Oh well, Jock's as good a name as any, better than some I'd been called.) The terrain was quite rough, but we landed safely, and on stepping down on to the grass, he explained, pointing, 'We're short of these in the Mess.'

'These' were mushrooms, growing in abundance all around us, but it did cross my mind, while I helped him to gather some, that *I* wouldn't be sharing in the feast. The Officers' Mess was forbidden to the non-commissioned.

There were rumours of going overseas, America, South Africa, maybe somewhere exotic, and I must admit to a slight disappointment on being told that my next posting was RAF College, Cranwell. At the same time, I couldn't help feeling honoured, if that were possible at 22-years-old, because Cranwell was (and still is, for that matter) the Mecca of the RAF.

We now had Master aircraft powered by 850 h.p. Hercules engines. The Tiger Moth was a very forgiving machine and, of course, a biplane – the Master wasn't. In retrospect, I admire the choice, as a step towards a fully-fledged fighter had become clearly necessary – cockpit checks were essential and I recall them now as TMPFFG (Trim, Mixture, Pitch, Fuel, Flaps and Gills). As was only to be expected, it was hard going. Studies in all subjects were intensified – meteorology, navigation, engine performances of Allied and enemy machines, theory of flight, armoury and air tactics. This kept us with our heads down most evenings, but everything was forgotten when I passed out as a Sergeant Pilot.

I walked off with my feet scarcely touching the ground, my head in the clouds. It was my boyhood dream come true.

In those earlier days, a great deal of superlative work was done by NCO pilots. The attainment of wings gave a certain self-confidence, although we'd been taught to beware of being too cocky. Statistics would show that in the first hundred hours of flying a certain fear sets in. This develops into a know-it-all attitude which can be dangerous, resulting in low flying and beating up a house or such like. Thereafter comes a settling down process ... and then the real education begins. An adage used to go around to drive home the perils.

'There are old pilots and bold pilots, but few bold old pilots.' To further reinforce the message, an RAF magazine featured 'PO Prune', whose pet saying was, *'Get your finger out!'* Not in the best of taste in polite company, perhaps, but effective on the men for whom it was meant.

There were no finer tutors than those at Cranwell, and rank was now irrelevant. As cadets, we were admitted to all that was sacred in the Air Force and sat with high-ranking officers while a band played in the balcony. This integration of NCOs and officers was possible because our formation was solely confined to becoming fighter pilots. It was certainly not a general policy.

OTU (Operational Training Unit) was at Tealing, near Dundee, which was a Hurricane unit. I could hardly believe this. I had actually made it!

From one horse power to one thousand!

The Hurricanes were in fact 1050, but what was an extra fifty h.p. in the big scheme of things? This was a tremendous change from my dear old friend Rab, who had given me just one horse-power, but I still regarded him with as much respect as I did my new steed.

It seems that someone decided to augment, or improve, my instrument flying. I was posted to Wittering in Lincolnshire, an enormous bomber station. Could it be just possible that I had been transferred to Bomber Command?

On reporting, gingerly, I was told that I was to fly Oxfords. Like the Link Trainer, the Oxford had full instrument capability – perhaps even more than that! In effect, it was fitted with the Lorenz Beam system. It was a twin-engined trainer of modest performance, and although it took a good few hours of familiarisation, that was not the important factor. A beam from the tower was picked up by a receiver on a dot/dash system. On the beam, it gave a steady note; a slight deviation, and you were up into the dots, *et cetera*, which resulted in the canopy being masked. With the beam and the altimeter, however, a safe landing should follow; at least as far as the runway lights – the rest was up to yourself. The Oxford was as good when I left it as when I got it, and to my knowledge, no Hurricane had this system.

Much more sophisticated equipment was to follow. I would emphasise the importance of setting the altimeter, and correcting it on landing elsewhere – fog was nasty, and you had to ensure that your height was well above anything in your flight path. The number of aircraft that collided with 'high ground' was tragic. Clouds, on the other hand, could be your best friends – they gave the chance to disappear and to reappear in the right place. The sun or moon could be used to advantage, as I have mentioned elsewhere, and even during times of stress, you could not help but be struck by the infinite beauty of the sunrise.

Thrills & Spills

Apart from trivial incidents, my only real taste of disaster so far had been at Cranwell, where a Bristol Beaufighter had come across at about 200 feet and on fire. One of its two engines was well alight and this aircraft could not maintain altitude on one engine alone. It was also too low for a parachute jump. Sudden death of any kind is very nasty, but to watch the inevitable death of someone you know and be unable to do anything to prevent it cuts even deeper. It is not something you want to remember too often, not even sixty years on.

Another incident of note was the approach of a Master aircraft. Let me explain that what I've referred to as 'circuits and bumps' in familiarisation with any aircraft, amounts to repeatedly taking-off into wind and climbing to one thousand feet, during which flaps are raised and the undercarriage retracted. Then a ninety-degree turn to port – isn't port always passed that way, gentlemen? – then downwind before making an approach to the runway when the undercarriage is lowered and flaps put down. Nothing new in that…

The Master I mention here, however, was obviously committed to land but with no sign of undercarriage… it would have to be a belly landing. Fortunately, on this occasion, there was no more than a damaged aeroplane, but it was a lesson that I would never forget.

The fact that I was now flying a fully operational aircraft, which had more than distinguished itself during the Battle of Britain, was truly exhilarating. These machines were armed with twelve, yes one whole dozen, Browning .303 machine guns. There were other versions which I was to meet up with later. All previous exercises in the air were accelerated and brought to a much higher standard. Initially, a trainee has enough to do to fly at all, but to do it accurately is a different matter altogether, calling for even more than 100% concentration. The sheer power of these aircraft was awesome, and they could fly at over 20,000 feet – which necessitated the use of oxygen.

To prepare for this, six of us were taken into a decompression chamber and given complete oxygen equipment. The instructor now issued a challenge. 'I need a volunteer, someone willing to go in without oxygen – just to prove what can happen. Any takers?'

Always ready to tackle anything out of the ordinary, I said recklessly, 'I'll go, sir.'

It was *not* a nice experience! As the atmospheric pressure was lowered, I started to choke, unable to breathe. It had been explained that anoxia would bring about a partial truth drug effect, and it certainly did, or so I was told… after I regained consciousness. Somebody had asked me extremely personal questions, to show off in front of the others, I expect, something I wouldn't normally have answered. I had answered, but only to a certain extent, and the soul was not laid bare.

In real situations, it gets more complicated, however. A person taking off without oxygen gets good warning and experiences this choking effect, at which point immediate action must be taken. On the other hand, a person on oxygen and attaining altitude when the supply fails through fracture or other means, has very little chance of realising what is happening, and so, as absolute alertness is vital in a pilot, the oxygen masks were mandatory over 10,000 feet.

At this stage, there was a relaxation in what I can only describe as army-type discipline. Each of us was allocated to a flight, and time of flying put on a schedule. You don't have an instructor with you in a Hurricane. I'd say that previous training had been such that I found no difficulty in this conversion. A fitter and rigger would accompany this budding air ace to his aircraft. A check of control surfaces and the fitting of a pilot type parachute were routine.

I would point out here that a light flying suit was adequate, as these aircraft were temperature controlled. Once the pilot was seated in this superb machine and strapped in, a starter trolley was connected and on the shout of 'contact', the throttle was eased forward and the wonderful Rolls-Royce engine burst into life. It was now necessary to test gauges, particularly ignition, which, although in duplicate, had to maintain revs on each. Guns, however, were not armed unless for a specific exercise. It was then 'chocks away!' and we moved slowly forward.

The ground ahead was now blotted from view by the engine, and it was necessary to apply left and right rudder in turn to see anything. In the meantime, radio contact was checked with the Duty Pilot, permission to take off was asked for and, on receiving it, a further check of cockpit drill was gone through and the throttle eased forward. This required liberal throttle application and, as the speed built up, the tail rose and we now got a view in front. It was then full throttle.

It's noisy, but what a lovely noise! Not too early in pulling back on the 'stick' as I get that floating feeling. Now I'm airborne. Stay low to build up airspeed. Undercarriage up. Flaps up. Ease back on throttle and maintain steady climb. It happens so quickly. The countryside's spread out well below me now. Flatten out at 1500 feet.

I'd had some flying experience, yet the fascination never left me. The initial aim was complete familiarity with the aircraft from circuits and bumps to formation flying, through clouds or at night. Although there is nothing special about altitude, its effect on the aircraft is pronounced. On reaching maximum ceiling, the sky becomes dark blue and there is a floppiness in the controls. There simply isn't enough air pressure to maintain the weight of the aircraft, and a sloppy turn can mean a drop of thousands of feet. The Hurricane was rated at 18-20,000 feet for efficiency, but careful handling got it quite a bit higher.

Ground studies were lightened by things such as clay pigeon shooting, which was probably what led to my fascination with game shooting after the war. I have enjoyed this sport for many years now. It's a matter of swinging through, not poking, the deflection and, apart from natural experts, needs practice – lots of it. That, of course, is incidental, and returning to my narrative, gunnery was becoming quite intensive and the gun sight more familiar. As the Group Captain at Edinburgh had pointed out to me, emphasised in fact, the whole paraphernalia of the Air Force in war is concentrated on the accurate use of guns.

Unfortunately, there were tragedies. One Flight Lieutenant, while on altitude flying, apparently lost consciousness and spun in. This was attributed to, and accepted as, oxygen failure, but it was thought unlikely to have been faulty equipment. He had been in the decompression chamber along with me and with that rank, had considerable RAF experience… but not in the air, which is an entirely different matter.

In another case, I was more closely involved. A Frenchman and I set out for a tour of the Highlands and were heading towards Glenshee, not in formation, he was well behind me. Flying at moderate speed and at just above telephone pole height, I turned north towards Braemar when I realised that the ground in front was rising steeply. I banked right, opened the throttle and climbed. The heather was getting too close for comfort so I pushed the throttle 'through the gate' and even then had to bring the airspeed rather low to clear the high ground. ['Through the gate' is when full boost is used in an emergency, over-riding the normal throttle openings, and requires an engine inspection thereafter.]

Although my colleague was well in the rear and should have had time to follow my moves, I was horrified to realise, some time after I landed, that he still hadn't come in. He was put down as missing, but later investigation proved that he had crashed. It seemed that he had left it too late. This taught me to have greater respect for these mountains, well loved as they may be by all Scots.

Around this same time, during night flying, I was duty pilot and in radio contact with a colleague, when I could sense a nervousness in his voice. I quickly informed the Flight Controller who took over. It was obvious that he was in trouble, for we could hear him on the radio shouting at first, then screaming, for his mother. His nerves had collapsed completely. He had probably fought against a horror of flying an aircraft at night and managed to conceal it for a good while... but not this time. His aircraft was within sight and performing some very erratic manoeuvres... which ended in an almost vertical plunge earthwards. Then came the deafening explosion as the Hurricane hit the ground nearby.

Having to watch something like this was, fortunately, not a common experience, although as the war went on, it happened more often. The feeling can't be described as simple nausea, it's much more than that; a combination of things. There is sorrow for a young life lost needlessly. There is guilt that perhaps you should have seen his fears days or even weeks ago and helped him overcome them. There is realisation that it could have been you. There is fear that it *will* be you some day. All combine inside your twisting gut, multiplying in strength until you have to force yourself to stop being morbid. You have to steel yourself against such thoughts. If you gave in to them, you would never fly again.

As this tragedy happened only a week or two after the death of the officer who spun in from what was attributed to lack of oxygen, things were getting a bit grim, but there is no alternative to flying a single-seater aircraft on your own, at night or any other time. It was a pity that the tension it caused had not been realised earlier.

Shortly after this, I was flying near the coast when I spotted a Spitfire below me, apparently from Grangemouth where a Squadron of them was stationed. I made a 'quarter' attack to ensure that it *was* from Grangemouth and to see if the pilot was awake. He was! He wasn't the enemy but – I don't know how it happened – I suppose I got a touch of the 'killer' instinct for the very first time and chased him. The Spit screamed into a vertical climb, which I had no hope of matching, but he overdid it, stall turned and plummeted down within range of my guns. No, I didn't shoot him down. We turned and twisted for some time and I made a head-on attack – there is no quicker way to die. I was determined that he would break off first. He flashed over me, dangerously close... but no harm was done.

I shudder to think now how reckless we were – young fools, really – who had no idea of the dire consequences that would follow if we misjudged our timing.

These encounters with Spitfires were commonplace, but this was my first experience. Although it was early in my career to call it 'dog-fighting', it was bringing home to me the relative abilities of the two aircraft and, if things were getting slightly dull, there was no harm in popping across to Grangemouth and dropping some toilet rolls. Innocent fun on these occasions!

Despite my original lesson in stupidity, a similar encounter with a naval aircraft resulted in the navigator baling out. Several of us visited him in Dundee Infirmary, where he was being treated for a bad leg break, inflicted when he touched down astride a fence with considerable drift. He said that as the aircraft closed, his pilot must have rammed the stick forward to avoid instant death and had inadvertently jettisoned *him*.

In all, we lost three aircraft at Tealing, another was damaged, and it was affecting morale, although a pep talk from the MO did go a little way to lightening our spirits. After warning us of the sins of the flesh, he concluded, 'Come and see me at the first sign of anything suspicious, even if it just turns out to be lipstick.'

Let me explain. ET (Early Treatment) was always emphasised if anyone had doubts about having contacted venereal disease. This meant washing with an antiseptic solution, which would have removed all traces of 'inflammation' if it was in fact only cosmetics.

I enjoyed my trips to Dundee. The Castle Bar near the harbour, with its partitions, was one of the favourites. Hard drinking was out of the question though, as Hurricanes and hangovers do not mix. It was not the first time that I had been in this environment, but it did equate with the doctor's warning, as all sorts of sexual behaviour was carried out in the snug alcoves. It deepened my fear of VD – syphilis was still an incurable disease – and one of these ladies would probably accommodate several customers in an evening.

I did meet up with a girl in the Palais, and we kept company for the remainder of my stay, although I had the shock of my life during our first meeting. I had asked her name early on – I'll say Jean for the sake of anonymity – but towards the end of the evening, I said, 'What kind of job do you have?'

She had already told me she wasn't in any of the services, and I mean... Well, it was a run-of-the-mill question, and I was expecting a run-of-the-mill answer ... Typist, shop assistant, nurse, the normal things girls do... but...

'I work in an undertaker's,' she stated, without batting an eyelid.

This rather took my breath away, poured a bucket of water over the panting dog, so to speak, but I managed to croak, 'In the office?' I fervently hoped so. The alternative was too awful to contemplate.

Jean shook her head and grinned. 'No, not in the office.'

Suspecting that she must help with the embalming, my blood ran cold, and I asked no further in case she went into the gory details. But she was a pretty girl with short blonde hair and baby blue eyes and we'd been getting along quite nicely, so I ignored my distaste for her occupation and saw her home. Her goodnight kisses were such that I asked her out again, then had nightmares about coffins and bodies.

A few dates later Jean asked me to meet her at her work, because she'd to work late to finish lining a coffin that had to be ready the following day, which cast a different light on matters. I felt much easier about what she did, and went inside her workplace quite happily to wait the half hour she said it would take her to be ready to leave.

I must admit that I didn't feel entirely at ease while I stood there, but it was raining outside. I was quite relieved that Jean didn't say much until she finished her task – the atmosphere wasn't exactly conducive to small talk. Anyway, when she at last laid aside the tools of her trade and we opened the door to leave, it was coming down cats and dogs.

As she said, with admirable logic in the face of this setback to our plans, 'We'll be soaked if we go out in that.'

Perforce, then, we stayed there for the rest of the evening. In case you are interested, there are worse places to be on a rainy night than a funeral parlour. I discovered that a coffin is really quite comfortable when it's lined and it was possible that the soft sensuous feel of the satin-covered padding acted as an unusual aphrodisiac. Better still, I also found that it was absolutely impossible for two people to lie side by side in such a container. That was a bonus in the circumstances, wasn't it?

Life and death…

I must ask forgiveness if my behaviour at that time seems irreverent, and my only excuse is that there was nowhere else to sit. Have you never noticed the absence of seats in a funeral parlour? I can't even remember now if I took my shoes off.

Back at Tealing, I was to learn yet another lesson. I taxied out one day, turned into wind and opened up. The plane seemed sluggish and I was heading for a clump of trees too quickly for my liking but not quickly enough to get off the ground. The engine note was wrong – the airscrew was in coarse pitch! Revs in these engines were controlled by the setting of the pitch or angle of the airscrew to accommodate the throttle setting. I was virtually in high gear – no use for take-off, and I passed over those trees with very little to spare.

Please do not think that we were oblivious to what was going on in other places. Air raids were taking their toll and the war on the ground was not good. These experiences have been related by many, but I was anxious to do what little I could, and I didn't have to wait very long. I had done over two hundred hours' flying by this time and was getting great satisfaction from it. The training was finished – but the learning had just begun.

First, though, it was home on leave. As always, it was good to be back, but things were difficult for my family. All that was coming into the house was Mother's widow's pension and my sister's wage, so it was a case of having to manage. It gave me great satisfaction, therefore, to be able to help out a little, since I was now on a Sergeant's pay with extra flying allowance. Just the same, I somehow found it difficult to settle, and I must admit that I was overjoyed when I received a communication to report to CO 534 Squadron, 11 Group at Tangmere near Chichester.

Train journeys were now becoming part and parcel of life, a commonplace occurrence yet rather uncomfortable. Boarding at Aberdeen, the terminus, meant that a seat was more or less secure, whereas those who came on only a few stops down the line might have to stand all the way to London. I was glad to sit down, having walked over a mile from Mid Stocket Road to Guild Street with my kitbag, loaded with goodies from my mother. Rab would have been handy, but at least in the RAF I was no longer weighed down by a rifle and sword.

Departures were usually about 6 a.m., an unearthly hour of the morning, and I hadn't expected anyone to see me off. In fact, I was relieved not to be involved in any tearful goodbyes, as a number of others obviously were – girlfriends or wives, I suppose, of which I had neither.

That particular train must have stopped at every station bar none, but I was beginning to feel quite settled down as it left Stonehaven... I had just another 600 miles or so to go. My mind went back to previous journeys when war was just a possibility, before the horror of Dunkirk and the legend of the Battle of Britain. This led to wishing that I'd been one of 'The Few', but I'd been undergoing a different type of training at the time.

The seats didn't take long to fill and on some occasions – the toilets, for instance, when one graciously gave way to the gentler sex – a pair of black-clad shapely legs, ending in neat shoes, was much preferable to the rough trousers and heavy boots of the male extremities. By day or by night there was the inevitable stop engendered by an air raid. The silhouette of that arched bridge at Newcastle is engraved in my memory, when a journey could last much longer than anticipated.

A change at King's Cross for the West Country was a welcome break, made even more cheerful by the angels from the Salvation Army, who refused payment for a steaming mug of tea and a 'wad'.

I knew that the aerodrome at Tangmere was only a few miles from Chichester in Sussex and as the train crawled westwards I prayed that 534 was a Hurricane Squadron. I was prepared to be disappointed, so you can imagine my joy when I reached the camp and saw several of these machines on the runways. My credentials were thoroughly checked at the guard-house... and then I entered the 'hallowed ground'.

INTO ACTION AT TANGMERE

This was Battle of Britain country and Tangmere was still quite a busy place. I was delighted to see the Hurricanes... but black? The explanation was simple. This was a night fighter unit which included Bostons, and I must add a little about this combination, because, to this day, I have found few who have ever heard of what were known as 'Turbinlite' units. This didn't mean that we flew only at night, but the operational emphasis *was* on night sorties.

The Boston was an American twin-engined aircraft similar to our Bristol Blenheim. It was stripped and loaded with powerful batteries, which operated a radar set and a searchlight situated in the clear Perspex of the nose. The Hurricanes were IIB and IIC specifications. The former had twelve machine guns while the latter was armed with four 20mm cannons – a fearsome firepower.

I had no difficulty settling in here. The CO was a gentleman whose array of medals was most impressive. I was assigned to 'B' flight with Flight Lieutenant 'Taps', DFC and Bar (I never found out his proper name). I got on very well with the ground crew – Fitter, Rigger and Armourer, all of whom I would be very glad to see on later occasions. The idea was that a Hurricane would formate on either side of the Boston which had been fitted with a strip light along the wings. Take off was in formation and usually fairly uneventful.

Bad weather did make it more difficult – and we were only a few feet from the Boston, which was vectored by ground radar to the target. On closing to within a mile or so, the airborne set could pick up the blip. A series of messages then passed, starting with, 'Cool', at which the pilots of the Hurricanes selected fine pitch to get as much flexibility as possible. 'Warm' was the code indicating that we were closing in when we dropped back into line astern. As the Boston navigator said, 'Boiling,' he switched on his aerial searchlight – which was absolutely blinding – and according to plan, the Hurricanes would shoot up the aircraft in the beam.

A Night Fighter Hurricane.

Our problem was speed, although the searchlight did engage several targets, one, I believe, being an RAF Stirling bomber. Fighter aircraft did shoot down enemy planes at night, of course, as they were meant to do. Need I mention W/C 'Cats' Eyes' Cunningham? Apart from being a fighter ace, he had an exceptional ability to detect enemy aircraft in the darkness. Moonlight was helpful, naturally, or the glare of the exhaust stubs, but cat-like eyesight such as his was extraordinary. In this era before guided missiles, the guns were fired at a visible target. Height can, to a great extent, equate speed, as a diving aircraft clearly attains great momentum, and the German ME 110s wreaked havoc among bombers at night, especially in moonlight.

Tangmere had taken a terrible pasting, but the brunt of the attacks had passed to the cities. Daytime raids on coastal towns, particularly Brighton, were truly destructive and bad for morale. The aircraft were mostly FW 190s, exceptionally good German machines. The tactic was to attain altitude over France, then come in at high speed towards England, crossing the coast at low level and lobbing a bomb into a shopping centre about mid-day. Casualties were considerable. In spite of patrols, few of these FW 190s were shot down – Hurricanes were too slow.

A New Zealand Typhoon Squadron arrived about this time (autumn 1942). The Typhoon was equipped with a 16 cylinder Sabre H engine and a 14-foot airscrew. Take-off was naturally hazardous as it was done in a tail-down position, otherwise the prop would 'dig in'. Once the initial activity was past, we soon got to know the Kiwis and couldn't help liking them – they seemed to be more English than the English (or should I, as a Scotsman, say, more British than the British?) Their photos of home showed how magnificent their country is, but there was nothing boastful in their manner. They had come a long way to fight for Britain, which they greatly admired and were not ashamed to say so. Apart from the Mess, the Nag's Head in Chichester was a favourite resort, and yes, we became much more than friends, not surprising really, since our lives depended on each other.

I had, in the meantime, struck up a great friendship with a Sergeant Nobby Bardwell, who had lived at Basingstoke. I say 'had', because his home had been demolished in an air raid, killing both his parents. He was considered to be a first class pilot, but went a little too far when he practised barrel rolls round American Brewster Buffalo machines. A few of these aircraft were stationed at Tangmere, and much has been said, still is, about them. They weighed five tons, needed a ladder to get into and looked like aerial tanks. Their performance was poor, and this was especially evident if you were rolling round one. 'Rolling round' is a manoeuvre requiring considerable skill, particularly when there is an aircraft in the centre of it. As I have said about the time when you 'press the trigger', guns were fired almost daily. Practice for this was done on smoke flares floating in the Channel.

On one occasion, after peeling off and diving steeply, I opened up with rather devastating effect. The flare disappeared and a column of water rose straight into the air. I was too low and actually flew through the water making the machine shudder. Another lesson! The dive was too steep, levelling out too late.

Gunnery was practised on drogues towed by another Hurricane, and clay pigeon shotgun practice was encouraged. Shotguns were gifted and I deeply wish I had one now; they were the very best – Holland, Purdy and Dickson to name a few. Gunnery in this context stressed the need for familiarisation and deflection – the ability to shoot in front so that ammunition meets target. Distance is most important, so the guns were synchronised at a particular point. A speed vastly superior to that of the target is not desirable, as firing time is too short.

It may seem, in this day and age, that the use of a drogue was rather primitive. There was nothing else, however, which could replace the experience of actually firing live ammunition in the air at a target. I dare to repeat that the whole structure of Fighter Command was geared to the few seconds that the guns were firing. A two-second burst by this combination of 20mm cannon and .303 machine guns was something that nothing in the air could survive – but these guns had to be pointed in the right direction, and the nearest you could get to that, certainly at that time, was the drogue. A Hurricane shudders in the recoil. But I think that I am getting carried away – it was just a drogue!

Amongst Friends

534 was a happy squadron at work or play and I have treasured memories of evenings spent in the Nag's Head. It was after one of those outings that I stumbled into a bomb crater on waste ground on my way to visit a WAAF on duty at the telephone exchange. I still have the scar on my shin from that escapade. These outings, of course, were limited, since we were engaged on 'ops' most nights.

As might be expected, there were some unfortunate incidents. Several of us were drinking in the Nag's Head one night when some American airmen started bragging on a quite outrageous scale. We let it pass without comment, but when a few of them began to ridicule Taps' medal ribbons that was too much for us, because not only did they lack operational experience, they were under strict instruction to avoid it. Contretemps such as these were, luckily, infrequent... but still nasty.

This was my first real encounter with our American Allies. Were they oversexed, over-paid and over here, as was commonly said? All I will say is that the bugle blown in 1914 and not heard in America until 1917 was long forgotten, but it had seemed that they were prepared to stand by and let us sink in the early days of this conflict, too. To be fair, however, many of them were later to give their lives, particularly in Flying Fortresses on daylight raids. But it can't be denied that they were rather too cocky at first, and they did have chocolate and, more importantly, nylons, to bestow on the female population in return for favours. We'd to depend on flattery, laid on with a stick.

Betting was endemic amongst the Americans, especially dice. I can still see them hunched over their board, rattling the little cubes to warm them up, then with a shout such as, 'Mamma wants a new pair of shoes,' the dice were cast. It used to niggle a bit that they never seemed to recognise that a dollar was worth only about five shillings at that time, a fourth of a pound, but perhaps we were over-critical, over-sensitive and over-jealous of their success with 'our' girls.

Thank goodness company in the flight huts was always good. We'd come from so many different backgrounds, but I was always to be 'Jock' – and I could laugh when, after hearing some of my tales about my time in the Scottish Horse, they pretended to think that all Scotsmen ran around in kilts drinking whisky, with heather sprouting from between their toes. (For the benefit of those who don't know, most of us don't bother with the heather or the kilt as long as we have the whisky.) Joke!

We also passed our time occasionally by listening to the wind-up gramophone someone had acquired. It was put to much good use – and I readily remember many of the popular records of the time, especially the Inkspots' rendition of *Whispering Grass*. The mere mention of this song, even now, can only mean Tangmere to me.

The bawdy versions of *Bless Them All* fitted in well with our mood after a few pints, but for relaxation, there was nothing to beat the sentimental ones. They could tug at the heartstrings. *Somewhere Over the Rainbow* was a classic associated with more peaceful times, and *You Are My Sunshine* was a great hit in the early days of the war. Then, of course, there was our own Vera Lynn, Dame Vera as she is now, who could always bring a lump to the throat with her songs, reminding us of home, as they were meant to do.

I have never imagined that I was under more pressure than anyone else, because there was a tension within all of us that was better to be relieved, and music was one of the best ways of doing this. If it did take the war to bring about the atmosphere of camaraderie that then existed, at least it lasted throughout the conflict.

It was now November 1942, with all the adverse flying conditions making ops decidedly hazardous, particularly fog. It was on such a night that we were vectored on to enemy aircraft heading for London. In the melee which followed, our formation was broken up and I was all alone. It was four hours since take-off, I was running low on petrol and I was heading west when all electrical instruments collapsed. To have no instruments in cloud at night is definitely not funny, and a landing other than on an airfield would be suicidal. For the first and only time, I put out a 'May Day', which is the last resort before baling out.

It still touches me to think about it. The whole south coast was suddenly lit up by searchlights set vertically, and since I had been flying in total darkness, I was blinded by them because the light reflects on the airscrew disc. To my relief, they went off within a few seconds, except for one which dipped westerly to guide me. This was a lifesaver! My petrol gauge showed '0' and I had been consuming the reserve for some time, but I could also see an airfield lit up below me. It was Tangmere!

After a rather nervous landing, I taxied to my bay and there they were – my friendly ground staff. They had been convinced that I'd bought it – as I had myself for a brief moment – and we hugged each other warmly.

A Wartime Romance

By this time, I had met Pam, a WAAF with whom I immediately formed a very close relationship which, unfortunately, was not to last long. She had been brought up with horses, and I have no doubt that she was a good horsewoman, so, apart from anything else, we had this interest in common. She was in the MT (Motor Transport) Section, which meant that, on occasions, I had wheels. Being mostly on night ops – and you don't sleep during the day at that age – we managed to spend quite a lot of time together. She knew Sussex quite well, and on a visit to a small hotel called the Leather Bottle, we saw a very senior officer entertaining a pretty young WAAF in the lounge. It was getting late and I had the brilliant idea that it would be a good thing to spend the night there. Gingerly, I booked in – it had probably been as Mr and Mrs Smith – and as we passed them, we politely wished the officer and his female 'friend' goodnight and slunk off upstairs to bed.

It was some time later that we heard, not just voices, but ecstatic gasps from the adjoining room. Still, good things were not the prerogative of high-ranking officers; even a lowly sergeant can have his moments.

This was the first time that I had actually slept with Pam, and somehow it was different; I felt awkward – I suppose I naturally am. A sort of respect had become involved. We did have an enjoyable night, I can't deny that, but not as passionate as the two next door apparently had.

On returning to life at Tangmere, we saw quite a lot of each other, frequently in my billet – how we got away with it, I just do not know! To give you some idea of what could have happened, an airman who had been caught in the WAAF quarters, which were situated some 200 yards away, was said to have been posted elsewhere very soon after this disgraceful conduct, and he hadn't even reached the object of his desire!

I suppose I felt that the social gap between us was too great. Pam had obviously been accustomed to a lifestyle in complete contrast to mine, and I realised that things were in danger of becoming serious. It did not help much when she was commissioned Pilot Officer; the increased difference in rank made matters very difficult for me.

To sort things out, as I thought, I took her with me on a few days' leave to my home in Aberdeen. We spent part of one day on the River Dee, with me rowing a small hired boat, and I found it was practically impossible to avoid continual eye contact in such circumstances. I had given her nothing, yet she was obviously very happy.

She accepted my mother and sister as if they were her own and our few days soon passed. She was in uniform – she looked great and I could tell that Mother was happy to see us together. Goodbyes were said and we took the train south. It was then I decided that I would have to break with her before things went any further and got too serious, yet we were well into our journey before I plucked up enough courage to broach the subject.

'Um... now you've met my mother and sister...' I began tentatively, 'you'll see why... I shouldn't have taken you home with me. You've nothing in common with them, they're just ordinary...'

She went berserk at this. 'What difference does that make? I love you and it doesn't matter... how can you sit there and make excuses for your own family?'

That cut, deeply... I was ashamed. I wasn't using the already time-honoured cliché, 'What if I get killed?' I just couldn't see how things could work out between us, even if I did come through unscathed. I would probably be lucky to get a job as an engineer after the war, and God alone knew when that would be, but there was more to it than that. I was not at all overawed by her, but from the start there had always been this sense of... hesitancy, if I may describe it so, and I had never allowed myself to have unreserved sex with her. We did spend a further night together in a hotel in Chichester. It was a long night, but we parted in the morning... for good. Maybe I have made a rather long-winded story of this, but it was rather a milestone in my life.

Pam.

A BITTER TASTE OF TRAGEDY

I was due for leave again on 30 December 1942 and in the afternoon the flight carried out air firing on a drogue, which Nobby was towing from his Hurricane. I had landed, put away my kit and was walking along the perimeter when my attention was attracted to a Hurricane overhead. It appeared to stall, the nose dropped and I fervently hoped that the pilot had baled out before it plummeted into the grass only about 25 yards from me. I ran towards it as it buried itself vertically in the ground as far as the canopy. Smoke, caused apparently by oil on the hot engine, clouded my vision, but... oh no! Surely not! But it was! It was Nobby, hanging on his straps in the cockpit. Blood was pouring from his mouth and ears, and the revolver he always carried with him on 'ops' was protruding from his flying boot. There was no doubt that he was dead. As I stood there, dazed, I could hear vehicles approaching and, unable to face anybody, unable to make myself believe it had actually happened and wasn't some sort of nightmare, I walked slowly away. It was the worst experience I had ever had to face. It was personal; we had been very close friends, though that word seemed inadequate.

I arrived home in Aberdeen still confused and somewhat bitter. Why is it only when someone has died that we appreciate them? Once again, I could not settle at home, and even knowing that it would upset my family, I felt compelled to return to Tangmere before my leave expired.

I never heard any explanation as to what went wrong with Nobby's plane and I didn't make enquiries later about what had happened because I was sure that the CO had done all that was possible. He'd had a lot of practice.

SONGS, SECRETS AND SORTIES

The war seemed to take on a more sinister aspect for me now. Bomber Command's big raids on Europe were now on and Tangmere was a good diversion for damaged aircraft which could not make it back to their home bases. It was near the south coast and had a good cloud record. Without attempting to explain the intricacies of meteorology, let me just say that topography or terrain dictates the cloud cover in certain circumstances. This, more often than not, seemed to mean that Tangmere had clear skies when other home bases had ten-tenths cloud. Under normal conditions, a bomber would come in 'on the beam', a guidance system, but very few systems were still intact in these aircraft – what was left of them – when they came home. At one time there were three Lancasters lying at the end of the runway in varying states of destruction. The blood told its own story.

Most of these bombers had been shot by ME 110 night fighters, many on raids on the Ruhr. As most attacks were made from the rear, by night or day, the rear and mid-upper gun turrets, as on a Lancaster, being most vulnerable, because they were the ones that could retaliate to any such attack. German fighters – usually ME 109s or 110s [twin-engined machines] – were as well armed as any Hurricane or Spitfire.

Although I had no experience of night operations in these bombers, those who had would describe a German defensive system that took its toll. It was known as 'coning'. This would amount to a searchlight battery scanning the sky until an aircraft was illuminated. A master beam, which was coloured, would then lock-on to this unfortunate bomber on which others would then concentrate while anti-aircraft guns opened up.

When one of these magnificent machines approached, it was awful to realise that the pilot was probably wondering if the brakes would work, or the undercarriage come down. He might even have to decide on a belly-landing; causing a shower of sparks that could ignite leaking petrol and consume the aircraft – and him – in a ball of fire. It was heart-rending to watch until he came down safely... or otherwise.

Obviously, these casualties coincided with the heavy raids.

It wasn't all gloom and doom, however, thank goodness. There were lighter moments, but I had taken to drinking more. Obviously, the messes of all ranks are licensed, and what had been a pint of beer could become a 'Horse's Neck', a mixture of whisky and brandy, and at a more reasonable price than in the pub. By this time, the Inkspots and *Whispering Grass* had been ousted by *You Are My Sunshine* or, a favourite, the *Wheel*. This went:-

> 'Round and round went the bloody great wheel,
> In and out went the balls of steel,

Or, to the tune of *My Bonnie Lies Over The Ocean* ...

> A young aviator lay dying,
> At the close of a bright summer's day.
> To his comrades who gathered around him,
> These last dying words he did say:
>
> Take the piston rod out of my backbone,
> Take the sprockets from out of my brain,
> Take the camshaft from out of my kidneys,
> And assemble the old kite again...

These were good-humoured evenings, often on the boisterous side but seldom ruined by drunkenness, and I understand that it was the long-established pledge of the services that all damages would be made good. The mess was almost a holy place, although that seems something of a contradiction. Invited guests were always treated with respect, and little did I think then that I would be similarly treated by the Luftwaffe in the not-too-distant future. It is just as well that we don't know what lies ahead of us...

To my knowledge, all RAF stations had bicycles, airmen for the use of, because even the petrol in the officers' MGs could run out. Mind you, it was strange how the 100-octane aviation fuel seemed to suit most of them. On one particular evening, four of us were returning from Chichester, bikes the order of the day, and although the road was not wide enough for it, we persisted in riding abreast of each other. Thankfully, it was light until quite late at the time and, in any case, traffic was not a problem back then. They say that you never forget how to ride a bike – this is definitely not true! Several of us had nasty spills before we got into the hang of it again, with bruises on various parts of our anatomies to prove it.

We must have taken a wrong turning somewhere and were nearing a hangar when our way was suddenly blocked by an RAF sergeant. No half-jocular 'Who Goes there?', 'Pass friend', and my presumption that this was some sort of sick joke came to an abrupt ending when he drew his revolver and said, officiously, 'This hangar is sealed off, and I am prepared to shoot if you do not leave the area now.'

It was then that I caught a glimpse of a Lysander aircraft with an unusual amount of activity around it. Guessing by the sergeant's manner that whatever was going on must be in the 'Top Secret' category, we had the good sense to obey him and about turn. It was years before the information was released that some aircraft had been engaged in under-cover flights to France at that time, and it was only then that I realised what we had almost stumbled upon. The Lysander was known to have short take-off and landing characteristics, which made it an ideal choice for such exploits.

It was also about this time that relations with the Americans became more agreeable and our Squadron was told that we had been granted honorary membership of the American Eagle Club in London. The airmen involved in this were pilots who had not waited for America to declare war but had themselves formed the Eagle Squadron in order to do something to help Britain and its allies. They were a fine set of lads... and their coffee was absolutely delicious! The accommodation was luxurious and they lived as only Americans could do at the time.

It was during these visits and other evenings in town that we more fully understood how desperate conditions were in London. The destruction was horrific, but again it was the personal angle that got home to us. The platforms in the Underground were a pitiful sight and not always safe, as bombs were known to break through to the stations and burst below ground with devastating effect. I am fully aware that this has been well documented – I have read most of the accounts and can vouch for their veracity – but no one who didn't witness it, can really appreciate what these poor people had to go through.

Back at Tangmere 'Ops' carried on as usual, but our weakness lay in the break-up of the formation on sighting a target, and there was no way that it could be reformed. Also, we had no idea where we were when 'the light went out'. On one such occasion, I was abruptly 'lit up' by searchlights and, believe it or not, I was flying through Southampton balloon barrage, several of them above me, which made me climb steeply. Most centres of civilisation and vulnerable targets were protected by these tethered balloons at an altitude of about 2,000 feet to deter low-level attacks.

It would appear that the whole conception of these night fighters was meant to provide an airborne radar bringing us into immediate contact with the intruders, but all that was very far above my head.

The pilot and navigator of 'our' Boston were both subsequently awarded the DFC (Distinguished Flying Cross) while on 'ops' in Mosquitoes. This was a twin-engined machine of wooden construction – yes, wood – and one of the finest aircraft ever built.

By now, the Hurricanes were becoming dated and not much of a match for the later models of 'Spits' such as IXs and FW190s, as their performance was much superior. However, it was still with deep regret that we learned that 534 Squadron was to change its role…

My memories of Tangmere I hold dear. The Ink Spots, the loss of a friend, the battered wrecks that crash-landed, the ground staff I got to know … they would all remain for ever in my heart!

HURRICANES AT HAWKINGE

I was posted to 91 Squadron, an 11 Group PRU (Photographic Reconnaissance Unit) stationed near Folkestone at Hawkinge in Kent. What more could one ask than daytime on Spitfires? And I was made most welcome there. I was the only non-commissioned pilot, and also the only Scotsman, so right from the start, I was 'Jock' once again. The general operation was to photograph the Belgian/French coastline from Ostend to Dieppe with, of course, particular attention to harbours or any water where landing craft could be assembled.

Now February 1943, the possibility and probability of an invasion was far from ruled out. The Spits were 5Bs fitted with a camera behind the pilot. Some were of the clipped wing version to aid manoeuvrability, while the 6s, with extended main planes, had altitude advantages, although taxiing was quite different and somewhat unstable. The undercarriage of a Hurricane moved inwards while that of the Spitfire went outwards, leaving considerably less distance between the legs. But you had to admire this machine; more blind in front than the Hurricane on the ground, but the slightest movement of the throttle brought immediate response.

Hawkinge was a grass airfield, with the result that take-off was sluggish, but once airborne, the Spit came into its own, although my familiarisation flight did not pass uneventfully...

Undercarriage up, throttle back, gain airspeed and pull back on the 'stick'. It seemed to be so keen to climb that I had allowed the airspeed to drop rather too far. Although I was in no danger of stalling (when an aircraft will drop out of the sky for lack of lift), I pushed forward again and gave a sigh of relief. Now steadied, I set the trim and settled down. It felt lighter on controls than the Hurricane and behaved beautifully. Its armament was two 20mm canons and four .303 machine guns.

By this time, I was well out over the North Sea, which was rather foolhardy of me, as identification was made on a 'colour of the day' system and any aircraft approaching the coast was suspect. You will understand that a low flying aircraft seen on radar gave ack-ack gunners only seconds to identify it. More of this later. I entered the circuit at Hawkinge and made an approach. A powered approach is not desirable owing to the nose-up attitude, and the Spitfire was handling somewhat differently from the Hurricane.

As I crossed the perimeter, I cut the throttle but I was still too high although too low to sideslip. I was also too committed to go round again and touched down well across the field. If it had been tarmac, I would have overshot – there were no brakes – but the grass held me and I stopped … but much too close to the boundary for comfort. This was a feature that persisted for several of my landings, until it became apparent that I was coming in too fast, but, luckily, no harm was done.

Accommodation was very good, as was the food, and I even had my own batman. The mess was attractive if not lavish, but I had still come a long way since Birnam! The pilots of 91 Squadron were veterans of many air engagements, yet they wanted to know more about the Hurricanes of 534 Squadron, and I was pleased to accept in return their knowledge and the flying experiences which they passed on to me.

Hawkinge was within range of German artillery, but after the first round, a bell was sounded. There was obviously no defence against these attacks, as their guns were deeply embedded in rock formations. Another feature was fog. I understand that this was a combination of smog from London and the sea mist known as the 'Hawkinge Horror'. If caught out in it, it was advisable to lose height over the sea then pick out a landmark, head for Folkestone with wheels and flaps down to minimise speed, and literally hedgehop along the road home.

Yes, I found a 'Nag's Head' in Folkestone. I suppose memories of Chichester were still fresh, but there was a good dance floor and although I was no expert, I found, like most others, that after a few drinks, dancing comes naturally, the limbs respond to the rhythm of the music. Too small to attract the big bands, the music there was practically just as good, and tunes such as *In the Mood* were to become very famous.

In the flying hut one day, I noticed a type of flying boot, which I had never seen before. 'Where did they come from?' I asked, enviously, hoping that they weren't too expensive to buy.

'Don't you have a pair?' was all the reply I got.

It seemed that all pilots of 91 Squadron were entitled to these Nuffield escape boots – black leather as usual, fur lined, but with a difference. The leg section was stitched to the boot in such a manner that it could be torn off in the event of finding oneself in enemy territory. Footwear would be essential, but not as conspicuous as the usual flying boot. Lord Nuffield had been good enough to provide for this. There was more – a beer tankard was also presented to me by the officers in suitable ceremony. It was inscribed, 'Presented to the Pilots of 91 (Nigeria) Squadron by the Colony of Nigeria', and I still treasure it.

After a few days, I was detailed for a dawn patrol with a much more experienced pilot, and in this respect, aerial combat had scarcely changed since *Hell's Angels*. The Hun could still be in the sun and come in on you unseen. We were to take off in formation, climb steadily to 2000 feet then go into a powered descent towards Calais, one to break off right to Dieppe, the other left to Ostend. There was some ack-ack but not the black smoke of the powerful 88mm. This was a versatile weapon, similar to our 3.7, which could be used at low elevation, even as anti-tank. It burst into black smoke – which made it, to me at least, easily distinguishable from any other shell – and it could reach 30,000 feet. The cameras were, of course, remote controlled, and with a slight dip of the starboard wing, good pictures were obtained.

Speed was kept high otherwise I'd have been a sitting duck. I must admit to a sense of nervousness, yet I shouldn't be ashamed of this. Fear is an essential ingredient in such situations. It increases adrenaline and thereby helps to effect the instant reaction that is necessary. As had been emphasised in all combat training, complacency is usually, even inevitably, fatal. Although one can boast about the 'good times', a rather high degree of physical fitness was needed, and only those who were truly fit would excel.

I was alone on this patrol and surprised at the absence of 'bandits', although the flight along the French coast lasted only half an hour. I came to have great respect for the Luftwaffe, but there was an apparent reluctance to engage Spitfires unless with a greatly numerical advantage. Probably the Battle of Britain had something to do with this, although it was fought mainly by Hurricanes. I do not think that my lone presence intimidated them!

In addition to dawn or dusk patrols, the Squadron fulfilled whatever duties were instructed by Group. To cope with this, a standby system was in operation, ranging from 'immediate' to '60-minutes'.

Before passing from these patrols, I must remark on the exhilaration felt, particularly at dawn. The air is still, the world seems shrouded in sleep and, as height is gained, the sun swells to a golden ball on the horizon. The engine seems noiseless and one cuts through space like a phantom. Clouds, too, take on a cotton-wool-softness and could be used to great advantage... but, of course, we were at war. Could this paradise-like situation be a scenario for death? Unfortunately, at times it was. Two went out, but two did not always come back. I suppose, in a way, we were provocative, asking for trouble, but as history will record, the Luftwaffe was kept too busy on the Russian Front at that time to be overtly bothered by us. In spite of the inherent dangers, I felt that I'd a natural instinct to fly. I suppose it was the ability to move in three dimensions. I did learn, however, that spectacular aerobatics were of little use in situations like these. An aircraft on top of a stall turn is committing suicide in close combat. First assess the enemy aircraft: what has he got that I haven't? What do I have that he hasn't? In the light of our radar being more accurate than the enemy's, I would say that the odds were pretty even.

Author with clipped-wing Spitfire.

The weakness of the ME was its high wing loading, a factor that British designers had avoided, and it stalled. This happens when the aircraft is asked to do something outside its capability. In this, the Spitfire was superior – yet to be in this machine and have to watch bombs rain down on our cities was a bitter pill to swallow.

'Sweeps' were still continuing over France. The 'black' towers, which had been erected to counteract these attacks, were about 50 feet high in order to shoot down any low-flying aircraft. Although ours was a PRU Squadron, it was naturally committed to all operations.

To attack all alone would have been hazardous, to say the least. Two aircraft were needed, and I had great faith in the excess use of the rudder in the approach, to disguise the line of flight. Various incidents occurred, and after one encounter with ack-ack, I realised that my engine was running roughly. I informed Hawkinge and asked that traffic be cleared from the flight path, as I doubted if I could make it. Thankfully, though, I did get down, and learned later that I had a broken con-rod. What engine, other than a Rolls-Royce, could have made a safe landing under such a handicap?

Those PRU sorties were usually eventful. I was returning across the Channel one day when Control announced that several 'bandits' were apparently out to intercept. On seeing a couple of ME 109s diving steeply with everything in their favour, I decided to make for the coast in a shallow dive, without realising how close I was. But I soon did! It seemed as if the entire south coast erupted, as every ack-ack available was shooting at me. It is easy to forget the 'colours of the day' with an enemy aircraft breathing down your neck, but the ack-ack barrage had a good side effect – the ME 109s disappeared!

While on another patrol, we were advised by Control that bombers had been detected, possibly heading for London.

After a quick change of direction, we discovered that the target was not London but the rail-yards at Ashford in Kent, and we got there in time to see the bombs blowing up the sidings.

Another of our assignments in the early weeks of February 1943 was to escort the Russian convoys on their way to Murmansk and Archangel. I have no knowledge of these ships being attacked while within 11 Group airspace, but our fuel was limited, and we had to turn back at a certain point. This left them an easy target for the Luftwaffe until further cover arrived to protect them from the waiting fighters, although it was very much later before I came to appreciate what those convoys had to face. Many of the participants were sunk before ever reaching their destinations, and the survivors still had the thought of having to run the gauntlet between German aircraft and U-boats on their return voyage. Of the vessels which did arrive at their designated ports, both Merchant Navy carrying supplies and Royal Navy providing escort, if they needed any repairs, they were liable to be caught up in the throes of a Russian winter, unable to leave the ice-bound harbour for weeks, maybe months.

Every branch of the armed forces, of course, played its part in the war effort. Every soldier, sailor and airman, and his female counterpart, was necessary in order to defeat the Axis. Civilians, too, did more to help in this second world war than in any previous conflict – those engaged in making munitions and war vehicles, the men and women in the ARP, firemen, nurses, ambulance drivers – not forgetting the Home Guard (better known now as 'Dad's Army'), the members of the WVS who did sterling work with their tea urns and sandwiches for the troops on railway station platforms, and, after D-Day, the ladies of the Church of Scotland whose vans, I believe, dispensed welcome sustenance to those involved in the fighting in France, Holland and Germany – sometimes parked just short of the front lines.

But I am getting ahead of my story. There was a long way yet to go before D-Day, and longer still, with many hard-fought battles, until VE Day.

A MEDITERRANEAN TRIP

The Author at the controls.

Hurricat, Algiers.

A Spitfire Over Malta

I was quite happy with life at Hawkinge. The other men had very much accepted me, but they were hardly the boys at Birnam. Some were married and others attached, which was not always obvious, though who could blame them? Even if this was not the desperate days of the Battle of Britain when life expectancy was sometimes measured in hours – yes, even minutes – we still ran daily risks. I must have matured somewhat myself before I could have that outlook.

On reflection, it may have been my earlier disappointment at not being sent abroad for training that was making me restless, although I will always appreciate the privilege of gaining my 'wings' at RAF College, Cranwell. Seemingly, almost all of the RAF cadets had gone to either Rhodesia or America after initial training; luxurious living conditions, no rationing, no blackouts, no war horrors. Their tales of beautiful flying weather and a perfect life-style may have made me envious, but whatever was the deciding factor, I let it be known that I was prepared to go to Malta – a tour of duty confined to six months because of the still-high incidences of casualties amongst pilots – and before long, I was on embarkation leave.

As always, it was good to be home. Mother was bearing up far better than I had thought she would, getting much support from my sister, for whom there was still no mention of boyfriends. On two occasions, I went to Hazlehead Golf Course – not alone – for it was here that my father, resplendent in plus fours, had taken me when I was twelve years old. He was born at Cruden Bay, a fishing village 23 miles north of Aberdeen, and although a small place, it boasted a first class golf course where golfers came from all over Britain and Europe, even

America, to compete in tournaments, or just to boast about having played there. At that time, the LNER (London, North Eastern Railway) had a branch line from Aberdeen to Cruden Bay, with one carriage provided to take those VIPs the few hundred yards from the tiny station to the hotel (also owned by LNER) and another to transport their luggage. This hotel was a palatial granite building established to cater for the highest in the land, but sadly, when Beeching made his drastic cuts, he dealt a fatal blow to the golfing fraternity by closing down this line. Perhaps the after-effects of the war had something to do with that, of course, also the growing number of car owners who didn't have to rely on a train to get them there. Whatever the reason, the hotel was closed, and after standing forlornly empty for some years, it was eventually pulled down. Absolute sacrilege!

The course itself, however, is still a well-known venue for lovers of the game, and a new hotel is to be built… but not by any railway company, and likely not in granite. Far too expensive.

In case you are wondering why I am linking Hazlehead with Cruden Bay, let me explain. As a lad, I had to be taught how to swing a club, and this local course was easier, and cheaper, to reach (there were, are, others in the city, but I still feel that Hazlehead out-classes them). I certainly spent many a happy hour there with my father.

These memories flashed back as I looked over Aberdeen from this vantage point, seeing the beautiful granite buildings and church spires piercing the sky between the two rivers, the Dee and the Don, stretching to the North Sea – the Granite City, or as it was sometimes known, the Silver City with the Golden Sands – a view that was to spring repeatedly to my mind in years to come.

The Music Hall in Union Street was a popular place to dance, but it irritated me to see girls left standing who had obviously taken pains to look their best, and so I felt obliged to have a go, even if I was no great dancer. It sort of dawned on me after a while that there was a reticence on the male side to take part, a shyness that I had cast off a few years before.

It was becoming more evident while I was at home, that the war in Europe was desperate; the Russians were advancing, but with appalling casualties, the RAF was bombing in Germany by night, the Americans by day, both suffering heavy losses.

Seven days is not a long time, and they came to an end far too quickly. My farewell to my mother and sister was a sad one, especially for me. I had been told right at the start, at my interview in Edinburgh, that survival would not be guaranteed, but I had never mentioned this to them – it would only have worried them. In any case, why should I have told them? *Nothing would happen to me!*

Embarkation was from Liverpool, and on putting to sea, the convoy of about twenty ships with escort headed due west, and it was well across the Atlantic before turning south. The U-boats were still exacting a terrible toll, but apart from occasional gunfire from the Royal Navy, this part of our journey was uneventful. In fact, our few days at sea were brightened by the abundance of tinned fruit available, and other goodies which were very rarely to be found at home unless through the black market, which didn't appear to operate much in Aberdeen.

After a night of spectacular electric storms, we arrived at Algiers without loss. In the morning sun, it looked white and inviting. Not So! Apart from the seaside boulevard, the squalor was grim. The Casbah, especially, had to be avoided, and more so if carrying revolvers, because they were much-prized items. I hadn't led a particularly sheltered life, but I had never imagined such heat and dust.

A New Zealand pilot and I, while absolutely sober (hand on heart) had a most bizarre experience one evening. We were approached by two small boys about seven years old, who said, 'You like see exhibition?'

'What sort of exhibition?' we asked, surprised, yet amused at being accosted by two such young children.

'Exhibition!' they persisted in chorus. 'Very good!'

They were clearly in the habit of touting for customers for this mysterious exhibition, so I glanced at my friend questioningly. 'May as well find out,' he grinned.

The urchins led the way and we had not gone far off the main street when we saw a largish house with a queue of men waiting outside. Realising that this was a brothel, it angered me to see so many servicemen standing there, but we, at least, were bound for better things – or so we thought – and carried on our way.

After paying the appropriate fee, we entered the 'exhibition' which was nearby – a small square room where about fifty of us were crammed in. In the centre was a bench-type couch, and you can imagine the uproar there was when two women appeared ... stark naked. One strapped on a rubber penis while the other lay down. It was then that I noticed what could only have been a recent caesarean delivery, which did rather detract from the intended allure, or titillation, or whatever was the intention.

I believe that foreplay is not necessary when using an imitation, but they were rather slow in getting into gear, or something. This didn't please the audience and one drunk in particular kept bawling, 'Put some life into it!' which, I suppose, was quite appropriate. The action did accelerate, but a sailor who apparently thought that he could do better, opened his trousers as only sailors can.

What happened next was reminiscent of a Hal Roach comedy, although infinitely more basic. The recipient of the sailor's sexual climax scooped up his substance in her hands and chased ... not him, but the heckler! This was so unexpected that it must have shaken the inebriated one out of what little sense he had left, and the audience erupted, hooting and cheering as she closed in on him. The room being so small, she didn't take long to catch him, and to his humiliation, and our delight, she did not spare him.

A most unusual entertainment!

In the few days of our stay there, I grew accustomed to seeing humans and animals share the same hut, but sadly, we didn't come across any more dusky 'maidens' and I was not sorry to hear that an aircraft was now available to take an aircrew of twelve to Malta.

We arrived at the airfield in a sandstorm – not a good omen, we felt – but after a few hours, we set off for Malta. The island lay gleaming in the sunshine and I got my first glimpse of Grand Harbour. I was not too impressed with the view, because the island was quite flat apart from a small piece of high ground and the glorious cathedral, which was reputed to have had golden gates.

Malta, of course, lay in a very strategic position between Sicily and North Africa, and the effects of incessant bombing were everywhere, including wrecks of ships in Grand Harbour. This proved to us that after using Italians to support the conquest of North Africa, Hitler must have looked on Malta as an important staging post, and did his best – unsuccessfully, thank goodness – to gain control of it. Our plane landed at Luka, the airport for Valetta, the capital of the island.

At this time, April 1943, the remainder of the German army was encircled and under siege at Cape Bonn. Malta had not only withstood the enemy onslaught, but was fighting back. Our billets were good, but foodstuffs were scarce, and meals were supplemented with vitamin pills. An egg – if you could get one – cost 2/6 (two shillings and sixpence) – about four times the normal price for a dozen. Moving around in those days of settling in, we became aware of a certain mistrust between service and civilian sections. Was it not Britain that had brought this mayhem upon them? The Maltese had been victims of a plan in which they had no part, but, thankfully, although many had died, the use of caves in the rock had provided survival for many others.

At last came the big day when we were instructed to report to GHQ to be allocated to a squadron. Four of us were Spitfire pilots, the others Beaufighter crews. Apparently, these aircraft had sustained heavy losses in an attack on Italian naval ships. The AOC actually spun a coin to decide whether I would go on a Spitfire 9 or a 5. The 9 was, of course, a development of the 5, with advanced performance, especially at altitude, due to a twin turbo system and carburation which could counteract negative gravity. It also had a four-bladed airscrew to absorb the improved engine power and was easily recognised by its twin air intakes. I would be telling a lie if I said I wasn't a little disappointed when I became a member of 229 Squadron flying off Krendi with a Spitfire 5! Krendi was simply a landing strip on the west side of the island, about 10 miles from Valetta, and had been very much involved throughout the Siege of Malta.

The Squadron Leader was a J. White, and our Wing was led by Wing Commander Ellis. It was stressed that no means of identification apart from name, rank and number would be carried while airborne. There is more to this than would appear, as any knowledge of the experience of an airman, particularly flying hours, would be invaluable to the enemy, because a diminishing number of hours would indicate that the RAF was running short of experienced pilots, who may have been shot down, or taken by the enemy in any way. It did not take long for me to be convinced that I was very fortunate to associate with such men, in the air and on the ground. But I had also learned why the tour of duty at Malta was limited to six months…

I had now to get accustomed to line-abreast formation which could become a line-astern on a 90-degree turn. I heard quite a lot about 'Screwball' Burling, a pilot with several victories to his credit, who had gone home to Canada to take over duties as an instructor. No one should be proud of killing people, yet I did regret having missed the slaughter of the enemy aircraft which had tried to evacuate Cape Bonn. I soon learned that 'readiness' here wasn't just a case of lounging in the mess or flight hut dressed in full flying kit, it meant sitting in the aircraft with the engine running, and more often than not, we didn't have long to wait. Some Messerschmidt Squadrons were stationed at Comiso in Southern Sicily, within a few minutes range of Malta.

At this stage in the war, it was imperative that air superiority be immediately contested should any German or other enemy aircraft be sighted. On these encounters, there appeared to be an enemy manoeuvre whereby the stick was pushed forward in level flight – known as 'bunting' – into a steep dive. This was difficult to combat. The carburettor of the Spitfire 5 could not handle negative 'G'. The floats jammed the petrol supply with loss of power, causing the airscrew to feather automatically to maintain revs. Positive 'G' then caused a tremendous surge of power, but too quickly for the constant speed mechanism to cope. The engine went berserk, and the only remedy was to pull into a very steep climb in an effort to reduce the revs.

I had the misfortune to witness this at first hand on seeing an aircraft pulled into a vertical climb with disastrous results as the engine apparently seized. The alternative was 'wing over' to follow the enemy, but it must be admitted that in the initial dive, the Messerschmidt had the advantage. After several such encounters, I practised diving vertically on power and soon thought nothing of this manoeuvre, although I had great difficulty in pulling out. It earned me, however, a visit to the AOC, who told me, with the suggestion of a grin, that I had alarmed the islanders – the scream of the engine had evidently sounded like a Stuka – but he accepted my truthful explanation.

It was on this visit to Ops that I was a bystander at a rather tragic incident. There had been an engagement with enemy aircraft when one of ours appeared to be flying east, away from Malta. In these encounters, many miles are covered and on disengaging there is little time to take stock, settle down and head for home. It became painfully clear that this Spitfire was flying on a reciprocal course (red on black) taking him farther from Malta with no hope of reaching land. Obviously he was beyond radio reception and too far off for a friendly interception. His fate was inevitable – 'into the drink'. The phrase may seem callous, but it was only by trying to make light of events like this that we could carry on.

The weather was typical, cold by night, hot by day. I recall one occasion when my bare arm rested on the skin of the Spit as I lowered myself in. It was painful!

The strategy was to deny any evacuation from Cape Bonn, and if any enemy aircraft took off from Sicily, they were immediately engaged. It was on one of these times that six Spits were scrambled to meet what appeared to be a determined attempt to break through. We had reached about 10,000 feet when we met, and a classic dog-fight followed. I engaged a 109 and opened fire with no immediate consequence, but as I did so, I saw another 109 in my mirror. The sky seemed full of them.

I had to move quickly into a steep climbing turn to starboard with maximum 'G', a manoeuvre which should have given me advantage. This relates to the wing loading of the aircraft, as the 109 will stall more readily than the Spitfire in a tight turn. I then became aware that my engine was rough and that I had probably been hit. I resisted the temptation to dive; the speed would inflict further stress. My opponent, however, had been outmanoeuvred.

I saw now that I was overtaking an aircraft – a Spitfire – on fire, one of my own Squadron, piloted by MacPherson, one of my friends. My horror increased as I saw a 109 with guns flashing about 100 yards behind him. What does war do to make the thirst for blood or glory such that this German was not content to have destroyed an aircraft but kept on firing at what was by now a blazing wreck?

I screamed into the intercom, 'Get out, Mac! For God's sake!'

I was amazed to see a figure emerge and drop from the aircraft that went into a steep dive. The parachute opened as I followed him down, and when I heard messages alerting the Air Sea Rescue, I headed for home.

Mine was not a bad landing, but quite rough. I cut the engine and there it was, staring me in the face – a neat hole where a cannon shell had smashed through a blade of the airscrew. Close enough! Several aircraft were destroyed that day… and some men went to meet their Maker. This was bad news, but I was relieved to learn that Mac had been picked up more or less unharmed. A miracle!

There was another side to all this, fortunately, otherwise we would all have gone out of our minds. We needed time to relax, and it was during one of those times that I met Marie Louise, who was still a student, but appeared to be very mature physically. Our relationship was brief… but informative. Her nervousness first became apparent one evening in Slima when she spotted a priest in the distance.

'What's wrong?' I asked her.

'We are told not to… speak with… the airmen,' she said.

As the priest drew nearer, she turned and ran off, but I noticed, as he passed, that he was of quite stout build; he apparently had not gone short of anything. Having got to know the Maltese better as a result of my acquaintance with the girl, I became more and more conscious of this ground swell of feeling against us; at times it was far from subtle. Prices rocketed in the shops and cafes for our benefit, which was understandable to some extent, given that we had brought the war there in the early days when Germany seemed to have the world by the tail. Maltese casualties had been, and were continuing to be, very high.

I did meet up with Marie Louise again, but it remained a platonic friendship. I believe that, as a student, she was more interested in my way of life than in my body.

At the flight hut, I enjoyed the camaraderie of men who were willing to give their lives for their country… and did. I never, however, attended a funeral. It was either into the drink or into a big hole in the ground… and we were inured to it. Sorties of one kind or another were a daily occurrence.

It was now the early days of June 1943 and the fortunes of war were turning. The Afrika Korps had been eliminated as a fighting unit and the invasion of Sicily looked imminent. But there was a fly in the ointment – Lampedusa – an island about 100 miles south-west of Malta. If you have not heard of tur-

binlite fighters, you will have no knowledge of Spitfire bombers. You are not alone in this, because very few people had.

The Spits were loaded with what looked like an enormous
bomb, and the sooner it was delivered, the better. No, I am
not imagining this, nor inventing it to make my story more
interesting. Many Spitfires were fitted with bombs. A machine
out of heaven, you may think... or hell? I don't know whether
any other Squadrons were involved, only that, with the weight
I was carrying, I was going to have a hell of a job getting off
the ground.

But it wasn't so bad. Naturally, it took longer to become
airborne, and this was followed by a stiffening of the controls.
Height was essential, as the bombing would be done in a
vertical dive, using the gun sight as an aiming point, and if I
recollect correctly, from 15,000 feet.

It took only a few minutes to reach Lampedusa, and it
looked as if more than 229 Squadron were involved. I have
never known the strategy, nor if this place could have been
used as a staging post, but we bombed in line astern against
very heavy ack-ack fire. It is an unfortunate fact that speed
affects trim and the top needle was showing it. A hurried adjustment to keep the target in the gunsight – by which time
the airspeed was going off the clock.

Not a time to flinch or ease back on the stick... but vertical? It seemed that the wings would be torn off when I released my deadly cargo towards the centre of the island –
precision bombing was out of the question, as was wondering
why we were doing it in the first place. That would come
later, although the reason was a bit above my head. In any
case, I still don't know if I hit the island at all.

There are several tactics to counteract the effect of such
descents. A Spitfire is not a pressurised aircraft, but I had long
since found out that by yelling as loud as I could I kept the

tubes open enough to adjust to the atmospheric pressure. It was at such times that I thanked the RAF for the quality of its instructors. Ease back now… but we are getting too near the ground. The controls are rigid but my vertical practice dives stood me in good stead. Feet on high pedals, curl the body as far as the straps permit and pull.

It is painful and the inevitable shadow comes over the eyes. I am blacking out, but some sort of instinct keeps up the pressure on the stick, having gone through this many times before, but never to such intensity. I was just getting on an even keel when I saw Malta below me. I have often wondered what speed that aircraft attained. The controls were now normal, which reassuringly told me that the bomb had gone.

In the flight hut, we discussed our experiences and wondered if it had all been worth it. A Spitfire is not a bomber.

Of course there were casualties, including LMF (lack of moral fibre). This is a dreadful condition when the nervous system decides that it has had too much. It is devastating to see one of your own kind burst into tears and become a shivering wreck. Naturally, we tried to help, but even alcohol was not the answer, giving only a brief release from the tension.

War is far removed from cowboy films, where they kill fellow human beings without batting an eyelid and then stroll off into the sunset with the leading lady.

FLYING INTO TROUBLE

Into the second week of June, the pressure grew more pronounced. Meetings were held, followed by the briefing. It was, to my knowledge, the biggest joint operation of the war at that time, involving both USAAF and British aircraft, the former to take off from North Africa – a formation of Liberator bombers escorted by fighters from Malta – on 13 June 1943. The target was Catania, Sicily, which was probably an attack in the strategy to invade this island.

What immediately sprang to mind was the fact that we would be at the limit of our endurance. Rendezvous was at 20,000 feet north of Malta. It was made very plain that the bombers were to be protected at all costs. Overload tanks were to be fitted to our aircraft – not an uplifting idea, because they affected the performance, but so be it!

During the evening of Saturday 12 June, I went into Slima along with a New Zealand pilot for a bit of relaxation. We went to a dance, drank more than we should have, and somehow managed to end up in the company of a middle-aged woman of doubtful virtue. The evening wore on and, having no way of getting back to our squadron, we accepted an invitation to stay overnight with her. This did a lot to enlighten us as to how the people were living.

Her home was a cave divided into two sections by one of those fancy bead curtains, which must have stopped looking attractive some years before. Minutes after our arrival, at about midnight, the air-raid warning was sounded, followed by the 'crump' of bombs. This loosened dirt from the rock ceiling, which settled everywhere, and as if that wasn't bad enough, next came the noise of ack-ack guns, at least one of which must have been positioned just yards away, if our ears were any judge.

Imagine the scene – flashes of ack-ack shells lighting up the dimly-lit cave, the earth vibrations from exploding bombs making the paraffin lamp swing about and cast weird shadows on the walls. It was what you might expect to see in a film made to shock – but we were part of it. Our benefactress was anxious to get on with her trade, however, but my fear of venereal disease stopped me from obliging and, exhaustion, and the drink, overtaking me, I fell asleep.

I awoke a few hours later to find my friend lying alongside me in the bed, where he too had apparently collapsed. In the morning, our hostess again tried to arouse our animal instincts, but seeing her through stone-cold sober eyes was all we needed. After giving her what money we had, we made a hasty retreat.

Back at Krendi, aircraft had been fuelled and armed, and take-off was at noon. It was only then that I learned that 229 Squadron was high cover – a position that I thought would have been better suited to the Mk.9s, but orders were orders.

Little did I think that this was to be my last take-off from Malta... To say that I had enjoyed my stay would be somewhat misleading. Entertainment as such had bordered on the non-existent. Slima was, in fact, the only place where there was any amusement, and that mostly in the few bars. We all understood that it was because of this environment nearly as much as the losses of aircraft that the tour of flying duty was limited, yet the daily swims in the Med and the companionship of fine men – aircrew and ground staff alike – made it all worthwhile.

When I think of it now, I try to understand the conflicting emotions I experienced at that time... it was almost as if there was a tradition to keep up. My early days in the services had been eventful, but far removed from the actualities of conflict – it had been the phoney war, an experience that did nothing to prepare us for the real thing. The howitzers had brought recognition of what guns could do, but just in exercises. The RAF was different. I had achieved something beyond my wildest dreams, and I had done all that I could… I hope.

Engines had been warmed up and, as the Very light appeared, we taxied out. Certainly there was a degree of anticipation as this was the first occasion in which my paramount duty was to protect other aircraft – even in my insignificant way. However, there was more to it than that. From the early days, when I realised that I had a chance of flying, my attention was centred on fighters, preferably single-seat aircraft. Maybe I had shrunk from the responsibility of having the lives of others on my conscience.

Now came the testing point, although I didn't actually have time to think like that. Take-off was immediate and we manoeuvred into Malta formation – line abreast in fours. Grand Harbour slipped away as we climbed steeply, with a sensation of drag from the overload of petrol. As planned, the Liberator Squadron came into view in box formation, an arrangement for carpet bombing, whereby the lead aircraft's bomb-aimer controlled the bombing.

It was about this time that the Sperry bombsight was being developed and gave great accuracy. Although far from indiscriminate, the pattern in the air was replicated on the ground. The Liberator, I'm sad to say, was not the best of aircraft. Its bomb load was poor at two-and-a-half tons, and its armament was not as good as the Fortress, which carried the same load. In comparison, a Lancaster's bomb bay held ten tons.

As we headed north, passing Mount Etna, the formation had settled down on course for Catania at the north-east side of Sicily alongside the Straits of Messina. I could hear on the intercom that enemy fighters were coming in and the black smoke of the 88mm was getting thicker and closer. The bombers, which appeared pitifully slow, turned in for the bomb run. I realised now that I was having to fly on almost full throttle to maintain position, so I checked and tried to jettison the tank – but the controls had either frozen or my engine was rough ... it appeared that the ack-ack fire may have been more accurate than I thought.

I was now at 30,000 feet at the rear, above the formation. In the meantime, the Liberators flew on and, as I looked down, I saw Catania airfield and installations erupt in a sickening black mess. Bombs had definitely gone!

As we turned south, there was intense enemy anti-aircraft fire, but the position of an escort is very difficult and, inevitably there were casualties. One Liberator seemed to get a direct hit from an 88 and simply blew up – instant death for all on board – but I could not dwell on that ... not then, at any rate. I had already spotted some enemy fighters and then I saw a single Italian aircraft another few thousand feet below. I do not know to this day what prompted me to ask permission to attack it; there's no time for logical thought in such circumstances. I can only suppose that I had two things in mind, one, to shoot it down, and, two, by so doing, to thaw out my tank, which would enable me to nurse the Spit back to Malta, but what was uppermost in my mind then was to attack this enemy aircraft. I asked Red Leader (Squadron Leader Whyte) for permission to break formation and when he gave it, I peeled off into a steep dive. The speed was high as I pressed the middle of the firing buttons – cannon and machine guns – and saw that I had hit the Italian. Starting to pull out, I felt the Spit shudder, after which there was no response to the stick. I estimated that I had reached about 10,000 feet ... and that I had been hit.

While I continued to dive, the airspeed was becoming horrendous, and the aircraft was completely out of control. Then started a process of extreme Positive and Negative 'G'. The canopy had to be jettisoned by pulling a small rubber ball situated just above the gunsight. I tried to reach it, but the 'G' force was such that I could not raise my arm. Within seconds, this was transferred to negative 'G', thereby crashing my head against the canopy which still remained there. I was dealing with forces well above my capacity, and which I could do nothing to stop.

In retrospect, I believe that the rear of the aircraft had been completely destroyed, and I was held there in a state of utter exhaustion. I kept struggling for some moments, but eventually had to give up.

I was now in a vertical dive to destruction, and a strange feeling of calm descended on me. Death was only a matter of seconds away and strangely, I was not unduly bothered. Hadn't I seen others die?

What follows is utterly far-fetched, and I realised later that I had been hallucinating, for there, on the port main plane, was Pam, in uniform with her hair streaming out behind her in the wind. Anything was possible to me after the battering I had received, so I accepted her presence as quite natural. I could hear her screaming, 'Get out! Get out!' and after several such screams, a panic seized me and an appreciation of the fact that I was simply letting myself die.

The aircraft had steadied somewhat, and I was at least able to unlock my harness. The vision had gone and a sense of reality had taken over. I knew that, if I ejected now, there was a danger of my hitting the plane, and in order to make sure I cleared it, I pushed myself forward on the stick. I was jerked out and into the air like a stone from a catapult, my head feeling ready to explode.

A sharp jolt made me realise that the 'chute had opened, and I hung there, completely immobilised. The departing wave to the brave antagonist , as seen in films, does not always take place in real life. Despite being somewhat dazed, my brain was telling me that in this situation, a pilot is an enemy, and as such can be shot while he is still suspended in the air. My adversary, however, appeared to be content with the destruction of my aircraft … luckily for me.

Then I became aware of the group of people below, looking up at me. One in particular had his arm outstretched, and I could hear the crack and see the smoke from his pistol. I was sure that my time had come. I was now only a few hundred feet from the ground, which I hit with considerable force. A pilot-type chute canopy is only 15 feet, as a larger one would descend too slowly from high altitude, leaving one very vulnerable. I fell, got up, then fell again. I had apparently broken my leg, but I was still being shot at, so I senselessly tried to run off… gritting my teeth at the terrible pain. A machine gun or automatic rifle opened up as I tripped on a bush and fell into it.

Several uniformed figures approached as I lay there, praying. I fully expected to be shot – had I not been part of a raid, which had undoubtedly killed some of them? I was brutally pulled to my feet, and some civilians ran up screaming something I could not understand, but it was quite clear that they were clamouring for my death.

Although the man who had fired at me in the 'chute was a soldier, he appeared to draw back from murder when it came to the point.

It was with some difficulty that I was taken through the bystanders, who spat and lashed out at me with anything at hand, and the pain in my right leg was excruciating. I had landed near a village called Mineo – I found this out later –

and was forced through a street thronged with people, where pigs were scavenging in the gutters. The soldiers treated me disgracefully, perhaps to appease the crowd, but if they had not been there to deter the rabble, I would have had no chance of surviving.

It may be that I lost consciousness, because I have no further recollection until I came to in a prison cell… which was absolutely filthy. I was lying on some torn blankets and still in great pain. Later that day, I was forced to limp to a room where an officer – looking like a Christmas tree, he was so festooned with medals, ribbons and gold braid – signed to me to take off my clothes.

I tried to obey, but it was far from straightforward. I could not stand up to remove my trousers, which was a source of amusement to him and his comrades as I lay naked on the floor. None of them speaking in English, I could only guess that the purpose of this meeting must be to demoralise me by making fun of me and of the RAF flying badge on my tunic.

I was returned to my cell and from a window I gathered that I was in an Italian camp of some kind. There was a number of soldiers wandering about, then one who looked to be an officer gave an order, at which the recipient stuck out his tongue and ran away. I never understood what had happened, but it certainly seemed that discipline was sadly lacking.

During my short stay there I was allowed to eat at their table, not much of a treat. There were dishes of a substance like Turkish Delight, crawling with flies. I could not eat it, but I noticed that neither did they. Back in my cell, I was brought what was described as wine, which smelled strongly of ammonia and was undoubtedly urine! I was asked if I wanted a woman, and they were not pleased when I refused. I took it that this had been meant as a spectacle for their lustful gratification.

I slept little that night and in the morning I heard different voices, guttural German voices. After all the horrors of propaganda I expected the worst, but instead I was taken outside to a car and one of the Germans actually stepped forward to assist me. I couldn't believe it, but I discovered later that they were more respectful to their prisoners than the Italians were... most of the time, anyway.

That was to come, of course, and in the meantime, I was driven some distance to the aerodrome at Comiso in Sicily, on which several aircraft were partly hidden in bunkers – mostly ME 109s – and I was put in a small room with a guard at the door. The atmosphere was very different from the Italian cell. Later that day, I was told that I would be interviewed by the Group Fuhrer (Wing Commander) and I wondered what this would amount to. Meantime, I was quite well fed and had my first taste of rye bread, which, contrary to expectations, I rather liked, even if it was rather solid.

The Wing Commander looked to be in his early forties, and I stood at attention, which respect I would have shown to any officer of similar rank and wearing the Knight's Cross of the Iron Cross and other decorations. In very good English, he expressed admiration for the RAF and the fact that I had been flying a Spitfire almost made us blood brothers. He admitted that things were not going well for Germany, but that future weapons would change the situation and would get the conflict over once and for all.

(The Spitfire was an exceptionally good aircraft although, as I have said before, it was the Hurricane which had been principally involved in the Battle of Britain, but as modifications were made, it was not possible to exploit them on the Hurricane. The Spitfire, on the other hand, was ideally suited to the purpose. Air combat depends primarily on ground control – radar – to get aircraft into the right position, preferably above, but, of course, the eyesight of the pilot, or the ability to see before being seen, is also very important. As developments were made on British planes, so, too, were they on German aircraft. By the time I was shot down, there were Spitfire 12s and 109 Gs, also developed FW190s, which had caused headaches along the south coast of England.)

The foregoing was included in order to help readers to understand that both British and German pilots could hold the other country's technical knowledge in high esteem, and perhaps explain the (what many may think impossible) relationship that was to develop.

The officer now asked, 'Would you like to meet the man who shot you down?'

'Yes, I would,' I answered, truthfully. It would be strange, but interesting. This man appeared to be in his late twenties, and we immediately shook hands, but because I had not studied German at school, we conversed with difficulty. He told me that he had been on the Russian front, and added, with great passion, that it was hell. Russians had emerged from the turrets of stricken tanks cradling machine guns, which they fired in defiance at the attacking aircraft. Men who were burning like torches continued to shoot, and the fate of any German who was shot down can be imagined. He also said that, in the early days of the war, Russian pilots would actually crash-land their aircraft in order to get the pleasure of killing Germans with their bare hands — but we did not dwell on these things. The subject, and what it may spark off, was much too dangerous.

The pilot took me to his aircraft, an ME 109G on which there were thirty crosses, [2] and this, backed by the Iron Cross

---

[2] It must be explained that an air engagement with the enemy was considered to be an air victory in the Luftwaffe, and the Americans also seemed to

at his neck, proved that he had seen quite an amount of action. 'Would you like to fly my Messerschmidt?' he jokingly asked. In like vein, I replied, 'Maybe some day we will fly together.'

I was a guest of the Squadron that night, and as we sat at the large table, I felt quite shabby in my battle dress tunic and light khaki trousers, yet I sensed no hostility. Then the Wing Commander got to his feet and, in his perfect English, praised the RAF for the part it had played in the war, but addressing me, he said that he had told his airmen not to discuss the war and in particular, the aircraft I had been flying.

My leg was giving me a lot of pain, so I made short work of the schnapps that was freely available, and despite getting quite tipsy, I can remember being told that five of our aircraft had been shot down. German losses, naturally, were not mentioned. I have no idea why I had been separated from the other prisoners, but I did catch one glimpse of Wing Commander Ellis.

'For you, the war is over,' I was told at one point, but in quite a friendly manner. On the arrival of a JU 52, my victor approached and silently handed me a tin which contained his emergency ration of vitaminised chocolate, saying, '*Das ist nicht gut in Deutschland.*'

A small piece of information here, for those who are interested in statistics. In the duration of the war, Malta had 2537 alerts, and withstood 492 days of bombing raids and 574 night raids. This was why the island was awarded the George Cross. Axis losses were put at 589 aircraft destroyed, 234 probably destroyed and 547 damaged. Many, many lives were lost.

---

have a similar system in which the victories claimed were somewhat exaggerated, whereas we British were scrupulously honest. Unless we saw the enemy plane actually being put out of commission, we did not claim it as a trophy.

IN ENEMY HANDS

Prisoner of War.

FRIENDLY ENEMIES

Apart from the glimpse I got of the Wing Commander, I never saw any of the other RAF pilots who were supposed to have been shot down that day, and I was surprised to be told, 'You will be flown to Naples, and then to a prisoner-of-war camp in Germany.'

I can recall having difficulty in boarding the JU 52, my leg was now badly swollen, and I found it strange to be sitting in a German aircraft and hoping that it would not be seen by the RAF. To be shot down by my own side would be the final ignominy.

The approach to Naples was a wonderful sight. It was a lovely summer evening ... there was Vesuvius ... then I was seeing the city. According to the old saying, all I had to do now was to 'die' ... but not if I could help it.

I was also about to be impressed by German efficiency. I was met at the airport by a German officer and handed over to a guard who was to see me into Germany. For that night, I was put in a small room in a very large hotel, where only a few hours later, an air raid warning sounded. The crump of bombs brought my escort, who indicated that I was to be taken downstairs. The raid was heavy and much too accurate for my liking, but what option had I? Upstairs or downstairs, death would be the same.

The stairway was packed with soldiers and civilians trying to get cover and I was astonished that they stood back to let us pass when my escort ordered them to make way for me, a 'kranken fleiger'. Once we were in the basement, a bucket of water was supplied so that I could ease the pain in my leg. It was unbelievable, so much courtesy in such a situation.

The following morning I was able to see that the hotel was a sort of amphitheatre with servicemen going about their duties, most of them German. The Italians were overconspicuous because of their rather silly, flamboyant uniforms, which seemed to include every colour of the rainbow.

'You are to be interviewed by the Gestapo,' I was told, which sent more than a slight shiver down my spine. To me, and doubtless to most other Britons, the name Gestapo was synonymous with torture.

Once on the train, I tried to settle down for what promised to be a long journey but, thankfully, a compartment had been reserved for me and my escort, although I saw that no provision had been made for feeding us. The guard, however, procured a piece of ham and bread from somewhere which he shared with me. This was my first taste of 'black' rye bread, and it tasted quite good… maybe because I was so hungry.

A car was waiting when we came off the train, but I have no idea of where we were taken, I presume to a Gestapo unit. My interrogator was somewhat older than I was and boasted freely of German achievements. I was more than a little surprised at his calm acceptance of my refusal to give anything other than my rank, name and number, but I supposed he would try to torture more out of me eventually. Of course, his English was perfect and he started on a theme that I was to hear many times…

'Why do you fight us? We should be fighting together against the Russians.'

Taking my courage – and possibly my life – in my hands, I said boldly, 'But Germany is fighting an expansionist war, trying to gain territory from other countries, and it has to be stopped. That is why Britain and her allies are against you.'

Instead of taking offence, as I had fully expected, he launched into extolling Hitler. 'Before our beloved Fuhrer came to power, Germany was a ruined country. It was he who rebuilt Germany, he who provided work for all, he who made Deutschland a nation again and restored our pride in the Fatherland.'

But at what cost, I wondered? It is still difficult to understand why Corporal Schickelgruber had been given his head and eventually allowed to over-run innocent countries.

Surprisingly, they were not interested in my aircraft – in fact, they possessed a number of them themselves. I was shown photographs of briefings at RAF bomber stations, including the target maps of recent raids over Germany. Had I been flying a special aircraft, or one with specialised equipment, the atmosphere would have been very different... as I was to find out. In the meantime, I was left quite dazed when the interrogation was terminated and I was still somewhat bewildered when I was handed back to my escort.

So far during my brief spell, I had been impressed by the high opinion those Germans had of the RAF, in spite of the fact that we were blasting them to bits.

Back on the train, my guard seemed to be more relaxed, and showed me various features of his equipment which were new to me and, I am ashamed to say, better than I'd had in the British Army. The *piece-de-resistance* was his pistol, a Walther which, he proudly told me, was not general issue but had been bought out of his savings. It was made of light alloys, and although, many years later, such a pistol misfired on Royal escort and was replaced by a revolver, there was nothing to compare with this weapon, in my opinion.

STALAG LUFT SIX

My destination was Stalag Luft 6, Hydekrug, about 60 km south of Memel on the Baltic Sea, and first impressions were grim. The towers in which the machine guns were mounted stood out starkly against the sky – it chilled me to imagine what would happen to would-be escapees – and there was barbed wire everywhere.

I was taken to a comparatively small hut, which accommodated one hundred men in three-tier bunks, of which I was given one on the top. Most of the others there were British or Dominions, but there were some Americans, and all were extremely helpful in advising me of the routine... although their obvious first interest was what was going on in the 'outside' world, especially in Britain.

Having left Blighty some months previously, I was not able to give them much information on that, but what impressed me was the morale of these men, all of whom were aircrew of non-commissioned rank, mostly from bombers shot down in raids over Germany... and some had been prisoners for over three years! The camp was in two sections, each of which was about the size of a football stadium, and the other section was occupied mainly by Russians and those from other enemy countries – enemies of the Germans, that is.

Appel was at 9am when the Commandant greeted us with 'Good morning, gentlemen,' to which we replied, 'Good morning, sir.' These roll-calls were also carried out at any odd time of the day, for whatever reason, which at times seemed pointless to me, but I was to learn that rumours of intended, purely fictitious, escapes were fed to the Germans in order to antagonise them, for the prisoners had plenty of time on their hands. As we all know, idle hands, and minds, make mischief to pass the time, but... mischief in a prisoner of war camp? A bit dodgy, but it carried on.

Then the farce started – we were to be counted. The result never seemed to be the same no matter how many times they repeated the procedure. With hundreds of men being lined up in several ranks, it was quite easy for one or two to move... thus leaving the total a few short. This was done on more than one count, and, naturally, tempers began to run out. Officers became involved, and although the German language does not lend itself to swearing, '*Schwinehund*' was frequently used. It may have been, of course, that we simply did not recognise other oaths as such.

The last ditch was to put us into a 'sheep-pen' arrangement, which was more accurate. A shortage or two could infer that an escape had been made – and the attitude changed. Retaliation could mean a withdrawal of the meagre rations, so this deception was not repeated very often.

I soon appreciated that boredom was to be the real enemy. The camp was on sandy soil, making tunnelling difficult and, as I have already mentioned, consisted of two sections, with Allied air forces in one and Russian in the other. A third compound, a little apart from the others, contained the hospital and, I presume, German quarters. Food was practically non-existent and depended largely on the delivery of Red Cross parcels, when – and if – they arrived. There was an issue of some bread and potatoes as well as *ersatz* coffee which did not taste nice, but we were glad of it.

I was growing more and more worried about my mother and sister – who must have been told I was either dead or missing – and I had to wait a long time before I got a letter from them. Obviously, this was a great relief, not only to know that all was well at home, but also that they had eventually been informed that I was alive. As I read it, a strange mixture of feelings flooded in; memories of other days naturally, but what worried me was that I was having difficulty in recalling the layout of my own home. The separation seemed to be such that I was frozen in time – nothing else existed except my present surroundings.

Surprisingly, the self-imposed discipline was quite strict. Footwear had to be kept clean and showers had to be taken quite frequently. Of course, these and other 'rules' were adopted for our own benefit… a hut full of sweaty and other noxious odours would have added to our discomforts.

I gradually got to know my fellow prisoners. All had their own story to tell of how and when they were captured. Sergeant Slattery, for instance, had actually taken off in a Blenheim on 3 September 1939 *before* the declaration of war was broadcast, and was shot down in the Baltic that same day. More astonishing still, on his first Christmas in Germany, he was said to have received a personal parcel from Reichsmarshall Herman Goering. It seemed that during the war there were many instances of mutual respect which supported the theory that Germany was not primarily interested in war with Britain. On the other hand, tales of extermination camps were already filtering through, and no nation with any respect for fellow human beings could compromise with such barbaric brutality.

Maybe as a result of my own hallucinatory experience, I was somewhat intrigued to know that Nobby Clark, a confirmed spiritualist, was participating in a parachute debate, when each of four put forward a plea to have the only 'chute. Taking the role of Helen of Troy, perhaps Napoleon or Cleopatra, his delivery was forceful, stirring, and the audience was swung in his favour by his apparent knowledge and enthusiasm for his subject. He was awarded the 'chute against all odds, despite his opponents being well-educated men, possibly better than he himself.

I subsequently asked Nobby how he had managed it, and he said, very seriously, 'I have a spirit guide.'

We met occasionally, and I was further impressed by his doctrine of giving what he had because the recipients of his gifts usually more than recompensed him in other ways.

More of this later…

Hours were spent trampling round the perimeter, taking care not to cross or interfere with the warning wire which encircled the camp about 15 feet inside the boundary… sentries had orders to shoot anyone doing so. I must emphasise here that the difference between this confinement and serving an ordinary jail sentence was not knowing how long it would last – that was what made it so demoralising. Germany was far from beaten at this stage, and the consequences should they be victorious were grim. In these early days, hunger was a real problem for me and I was told that it would take about a year for the stomach to contract enough to be satisfied with the meagre rations we were given to eat.

However scarce, food must out, and the method of collection was novel. In a brick building about thirty yards long was the cesspit with a convenient beam for squatters. When the time came to evacuate the contents, a tanker would arrive. I was quite intrigued to see it stop near the building, where a large pipe was unloaded and connected to the tank – the other end was immersed in the pit.

What could only have been petrol was then poured into a container at the top of the tank. Next, there was an explosion sufficient to lift a heavily spring-loaded valve, which shut with a crash. The vacuum created sucked up the deposits.

Our Camp Leader was Sergeant Pilot 'Dixie' Deans, who was highly respected by us and by the Germans, and he and his committee made all decisions on camp conduct. As is widely known, it is incumbent on all prisoners of war to escape, and this was attempted by tunnelling and various devious means. Tunnelling was difficult in the sandy soil, so a type of pit prop was essential. This was done by giving up bedboards, while air was introduced by *klim* tins (powdered milk) from the parcels.

Of course, this had all been devised long before my arrival, and experience had shown that when a mechanical roller was driven round the area between the warning wire and the outer fence, it was heavy enough to break into any tunnel of which the Germans probably had knowledge by seismograph.

I understand that this was overcome by digging two tunnels, and, because the machine was always driven clockwise, while the first one to be discovered was being filled in, a desperate effort was made to break out through the second. I was told that eight men had escaped in this way, but unfortunately, all had been recaptured.

I must explain how the confinement in those camps compared with others. In the early days, RAF prisoners had been put out to work, but such was the sabotage they did that all had to be confined. Strangely, some of the guards (*Gefreiters*) had British sympathies, and friendships were made. It would start with perhaps a few cigarettes in exchange for little 'luxuries' – German cigarettes were vile – and as confidences were built up, they were persuaded to bring items into the camp. If a particular guard was unable to obtain what was requested of him, he would be given several packets of cigarettes as a further incentive, but unhappily, a senior German officer was told of this treachery, and after a search of one man revealing the cigarettes, he was transferred to the Russian front.

If a guard *was* able to obtain highly sensitive documents, such as ration cards, he was well rewarded with chocolates for his children in addition to cigarettes for himself, plus a promise of immunity from prosecution in the event of an Allied victory. The ultimate barter was his own identity card, which he was told should never be used, as it declared in bold type that the death penalty would be carried out on any person misusing it. Once photographed – with a camera obtained by similar means – it was shown to the guard, and his genuine identity card was returned along with one of the duplicates. Compromised, his life was thus at stake and he could refuse nothing that was asked of him. I presume it was by those same means that parts had been obtained to equip the radio receiver which kept us in touch with the outside world, and which the Germans never traced.

In this respect, another attempted escape is worth telling. The carcass of a horse had been taken into the camp, but because it was already unfit for human consumption, it had to be removed as quickly as possible, and, while it was being loaded onto a cart, a prisoner forced himself into the rib cage of the stinking animal. When the cart went through the gates, however, a bayonet was thrust into the carcass as a precaution. Such was the determination to escape, that all kinds of efforts were made, often in vain, and sometimes, as in this case, possibly fatal.

But even here, there were moments to lighten our despondency. Mason, an American who was later to become one of my best friends, had a habit of talking in his sleep, and occasionally gave lurid details of his close association with actresses he had met. Of rather humble parentage, he had been adopted by a wealthy family; his twentieth birthday gift had been an aircraft, his twenty-first the gold watch he always wore.

It is perhaps not widely known that starvation over a long period usually has a devastating effect on sexual feelings, which was true of the older prisoners, but not so the younger, especially not Mason. He was lying naked in the sun one day, fast asleep, when some observant fellow noticed his manhood rearing its ugly head. A crowd gathered, watching the erection and giving loud applause at the eventual ejaculation. This awakened the poor American, who was appalled to find a huge audience had observed his sleeping fantasy.

A large hut served for any communal activities. It could be used as a debating chamber, or as a theatre of sorts. On one instance, the leading 'lady' was a real smasher, and would have turned heads in any company. Unfortunately, a few Aussies had saved their sugar ration and, with raisins from parcels, had brewed up a wickedly potent wine. They plied this to the leading 'lady' and the last I saw of 'her', 'she' was running hell for leather between huts with said Aussies in hot pursuit. I never did find out if they caught 'her'.

THE CAMP HOSPITAL

The weather was growing somewhat chilly when a bad thunderstorm hit the camp, the lightning simultaneous with the thunder, and that is really close. One of the lads was killed and several injured; I believe that their bodies had been in contact with sheet metal.

I was beginning to come to terms with life as a POW, but I still had a lot to learn. A bed-fellow on the second tier wanted to change bunks with me to be beside his 'friend', but it raised no question in my mind – I had never come across homosexuality at that time. It was not something that was mentioned in the passing.

I also took some time to understand about the 'mespots', which were put up on the notice board. These were letters from home breaking off an association with the prisoner, an engagement or even a marriage. Many actually confessed that the lady concerned was having a child by another man.

One wife, who wrote that she was pregnant by an American, ended her letter by saying, 'Don't worry, he'll send you parcels.' Not much of a consolation... or was it, given his circumstances?

I regret to say that very few women seemed to remain true, but the understanding was that such letters would be posted up on the notice board. Why? I do not know.

In the meantime, I was beginning to learn more about chess, and another 'must' to keep your brain up to scratch was bridge, even if many of the declared 'hands' were assisted by tapping on the partner's shoe. Red Cross parcels were heaven-sent, but it was rare to get one to oneself. Most were British but some were American, the latter containing somewhat frivolous items such as sweets and cigarettes, still acceptable but not so sought after as the corned beef in the former.

About this time, I began to feel quite groggy, and put it down to delayed reaction to the vast change in my circumstances, but very soon, my eyes turned yellow and I was forced to report sick. The makeshift hospital was outside the main camp, although it was still very secure.

A British doctor, Dr Pollock, examined me. 'You have jaundice,' he told me, 'so we'll have to keep you in hospital for a while.'

I was unwilling to agree to this. I felt that I would be getting an unfair advantage, but Dr Pollock was adamant, so hospital it was. There was one blessing – feeling as I did, I had no appetite.

My condition deteriorated and the yellowing got worse. My feet were so itchy that I tore off some of the skin by rubbing one foot against the other. I was given massive doses of *Karlsbader* salts, as even my stools were yellow, and I was put on a course of intravenous injections three times a day. My pulse rate dropped to the low forties. I was very ill indeed.

This coincided with a proposed visit by the International Red Cross and Dr Pollard told me that he had recommended my repatriation. Before that, however, I was taken to a hospital of unknown whereabouts, and was allowed to see my pulsing intestines on an X-ray screen (not a very thrilling, nor morale-boosting, spectacle, but it was still quite interesting to learn how the body works).

The diagnosis was cirrhosis of the liver and I was confined to bed. I didn't fully realise how ill I was until, on one occasion after I had sneaked off to the lavatory, Dr Pollock asked bluntly, 'Do you want to kill yourself?'

Now came a nasty incident. Because a tunnel had been discovered in the camp, all bed-boards were confiscated. This included the hospital, where the patients, about twenty of us, were left lying on the floor. Most were suffering from gunshot wounds; some were in a pitiful mess. One American had been shot in the foot and osteomylitis had set in. The pus kept oozing from it but there was little that could be done. I learned that the crew had set off from an English aerodrome in a B 17 to test the compass and had been shot down over Yugoslavia. Yes, that is true. Another case of black on red. It may sound ridiculous, but in ten-tenths cloud, mistakes are easily made. Others had mental problems and could not come to terms with life, especially life like this. One poor devil refused to eat – he had what was called melancholia – and eventually died.

Although I was treated by Dr Pollock, there was another doctor by the name of Hay. I understand that both these men opted to remain with the prisoners, and I sincerely hope that their devotion was rewarded. Another patient admitted while I was there had parachuted into France at night after his plane was shot down. He was screaming that he landed in a deep ditch, and when trying to climb out was left with handfuls of bones from the First World War. I find this hard to believe, but it had completely turned his brain and rendered him quite mad.

By now, winter was approaching, and I cannot express my gratitude enough to the Red Cross for a blanket I was given. I must have been in a pensive mood when my mind wandered back to Forvie, an area about twenty odd miles from Aberdeen; or it might have been the weather that reminded me. Here is what I wrote:

FORVIE SANDS
The wind blows snell [bitterly cold] o'er Forvie sands
No longer there our 'bivvy' [bivouac tent] stands.
In that happy, carefree land.

We heard the lapwing's mournful cry,
The gulls shrieked as they circled high
Into a blue ethereal sky.
Some rabbits scurried here and there,
Nature's glories everywhere

But now the sands are cauld and weet [cold and wet],
The gulls have found a new retreat.
No longer do they circle high,
But scan a misty, cloudy sky.
The rabbits now within their burrows
The lapwing cries from snow-clad furrows.

But when that summer sun comes back
Off we'll go off the beaten track.
Back to Forvie's hills and dunes,
Where life itself plays careless tunes.

I kept that piece of paper, words penned from a heart aching to be at home again, to see that stretch of sands where the River Ythan merges into the North Sea. (This area – only a few miles from Cruden Bay, my father's birthplace – is now a Nature Reserve with notices describing the different species of birds to be seen.) When I was a lad, of course, it was just a place for me to go with my chum to watch the birds, to pitch our little tent for a night and be away from the cares we thought we had at that time. But all this is a digression…

A new arrival in a bed alongside mine had been shot down while flying a Spitfire 12, the Griffen, from 91 Squadron, and I envied him for having flown such an advanced aircraft, but we spoke long into the night about life at Hawkinge. He did not appear to be seriously wounded, and I never found out why he was in hospital, for, by mutual agreement, we never discussed our ailments. He was discharged before I was, and I feared for his safety.

Mason, the sleep-talker and fantasy-weaver, had been taken away for some reason, and when he returned to the camp he was unrecognisable. Every tooth had been twisted, some jutting through the upper palate. It had apparently become known that, at the time he was captured, he had been operating a new bombsight, probably the Sperry, and his continued refusal to give any information on it had led to his being tortured.

My condition was improving slightly, yet I was told I still had a long way to go. Nobby Clark had visited me once or twice, and although he talked about his spiritual beliefs, he didn't try to peddle them. He compared them to a radio, because the sound is there if you are on the same wavelength. On more than one occasion while I was in his company, he was approached by another prisoner offering him cigarettes and saying, 'I had a parcel from home.'

Cigarettes were good currency, and Nobby would say to me, 'Do you see what I mean?' because this supported his spiritual beliefs.

I found him very interesting, and was alarmed when, on what turned out to be his last visit, he said, 'I have to go back home.'

'You can't leave,' I murmured.

'What's to stop me?' he smiled.

'You'd have to outwit the Germans.'

'So?'

He was so calm, but I had to try to make him see sense, for his own safety. 'What are you planning on doing? Going over or under the wire?'

'Neither. I will walk out through the gate. I have done all I can do here.'

He *had* done a lot of good in the camp and had shown that man can be motivated by other than greed. He took me further aback, however, when he went on, 'I have been advised...' (by his spirits, I supposed) '...to tell you to pump some water.'

To explain – all our water was raised into tanks by hand pumps and the only way to obtain any was to pump it up. I thought the suggestion quite ludicrous, but during the night, I decided to give it a try, so I got out of bed and pumped for a few seconds. I felt slightly better for it (auto-suggestion?) and carried on with the exercise, increasing the time daily, and somehow, my health improved. I seemed to be on the road to recovery, but surely not by Divine Intervention? The doctor commented on how pleased he was by my progress, but I said nothing about my nocturnal exercises. How could I explain, when I preferred to think of it as a coincidence or whatever?

As for Nobby, he *did* go out through the gate – repatriated as a schizophrenic!

A senior warrant officer, who shall be nameless, also walked out this way... dressed as a German officer. The theatre costumes had been plundered as they had been for the 'leading lady'. It was later said that he became involved in forming a link to England.

The winter of 1943 was severe, and I understand that the Baltic was completely frozen over. It was about this time that I received another letter from home which, of course, was an immense boost to me. There was nothing of import in it – there wasn't room to write much – but at least it let me know that my mother and sister were well, and that they were thinking of me.

Escape attempts were made, but none as spectacular as with a Russian breakout. Men rushed at the wire, a second wave followed and climbed on the backs of the first. In this way, others got over the wire... only to be mown down by the machine guns in the towers. Those who did get away were captured and left in the snow to die. I can still hear their screams. It did not, however, worry the Germans, who had been indoctrinated to believe that Russians were sub-human.

Their attitude towards us varied with the conduct of the war. As Allied victories, particularly on the Eastern front, made their chance of winning look more doubtful, their manner softened against some of their 'charges', but as far as I could see, there remained this belief in a 'secret weapon'. Hitler had promised that there would be one, and his word was gospel. So convincing were they about this that we half believed them, and wondered what form this secret weapon would take... unless it turned out to be their dogs, who were trained to tear at the testicles.

I did befriend a Russian officer who was detailed for work at the hospital. His English was quite good, which is more than could be said for my Russian, although I did learn one word, which undoubtedly saved my life some considerable time later – *Tovarich* (friend). We did become good friends and tried hard to conquer the linguistic and cultural barrier. In the light of future events, this may have been futile, but he did manage to get one thing across to me. In his country, the aristocracy had been feeding meat to the dogs while the other people starved.

Christmas to me, that year, conjures up a picture of a prisoner dying of consumption. The snowflakes were falling on his bed, fresh air being considered essential for this illness, even in Britain, while from somewhere near at hand came the strains of *Silent Night*. It took me back to Christmases gone by, and I could not help but wonder if they would ever return. Perhaps I have not described my home in any great detail, but I ached to get back to it and away from this terrible, alien world.

As the weeks passed, I was getting that bit better but not allowed to leave the hospital, and at last, I said, 'Can't I be of any help to you, doctor?' I thought it was the least I could do.

Dr Pollock raised his brows and rolled his eyes. 'Can you?' he grinned. 'By God, I'll say you can!'

That very day, he started taking me with him on his rounds. One chap had a boil of enormous proportions on his buttock, and was obviously in severe pain, but all medical equipment, naturally, was basic. The anaesthetic was *Evapan*, a derivative of the truth drug, under the influence of which many tales were told. The offending lump was lanced by a deep cut with the scalpel and the pus that spewed out was almost indescribable. A glass rod was pushed into the gory mess and stirred as if making porridge. He winced, and when he came round, I asked, sympathetically, 'How d'you feel?'

'I'm in heaven,' he smiled, 'absolute heaven. No pain at all.'

I could scarcely credit this, but he appeared to be speaking the truth.

Another man had a carbuncle removed from his neck where it was twisting his spine, causing his head to lie on his shoulder. Puzzling over what sort of treatment would help him, I was told that such growths have to be removed without puncturing the sac… and this one came out intact, like a golf ball.

I mention these cases light-heartedly, which is how we had to look at them then for our own sanity, but many were badly wounded, physically and mentally. The treatment for most was *Ictheol*, a black tarry substance that made a horrible mess.

I boiled my needles and gave many intra-venous injections, extremely thankful that I no longer needed them myself.

There was another incident that made me smile… after it was over. An American had a really nasty leg wound, turning gangrenous by the smell, with a white core so sore and tender that he jumped whenever I touched it. To remove this, I fixed on Spencer-Wells pliers and pulled… It came out… and kept coming out for about an inch, and I broke out in a sweat, thinking that I had locked onto a tendon, but all I could do was keep pulling. I was imagining his toes curling up when out came a piece of electric cable nearly six inches long, which had been blasted into his leg from his electrically-heated flying-suit at the time he was shot down. The missile which had done the damage had been removed, but the cable had inadvertently been left behind. I was quite pleased with myself when the doctor told me that I had probably saved this man's leg.

Some of the arrivals at the camp were in a pitiful state. They had not liked to relieve themselves on the floor, and had thus become constipated… some for as many as fourteen days! Can you imagine that? There was nothing else for it but get a pair of surgical gloves and pick it out. It was not a particularly nice job, but very much appreciated by the men concerned.

Others were more difficult to deal with. Another prisoner, let's call him Bobby, had been depressed for so long that he was now suicidal, but his presence there took a strange twist when he fouled his bed and started to throw the excrement at anyone within range. One lump hit a rather large American airman called Rasmussen, who picked Bobby up and roared, 'If you were a big guy I'd hit ya, but ya're only a little 'un so I'll just clip ya,' whereupon he hit him a glancing blow, but sufficient to drop Bobby at his feet. I became very friendly with Rasmussen – he spoke my kind of language.

The war dragged on, but it did appear that Germany was finished. Allied air raids were reaching enormous proportions. Hamburg had been obliterated in a fire storm, in which the German dentist who visited us occasionally had lost his house and every single member of his family. Even the rats died.

In the camp, a man who had gone completely mad was to be confined in a separate hut and I was asked if I would stay with him that night. This meant, of course, that once inside our temporary abode, neither of us could leave it, because we would be shot if seen outside in the dim lights of the camp in the dark. He sat throughout what seemed an extra-long night, clenching and unclenching his fists while looking at the floor.

He flew at the doctor's throat when he arrived in the morning, and would have killed him if the two of us had not managed to restrain him. I was left shaking with relief that he hadn't had a go at me when we were alone, and to be quite honest, I have never understood why he didn't.

A FEAT OF ENDURANCE

As month after month passed, it was difficult to understand what was happening about the Second Front – Russians were dying in millions, but the advance continued. This, however, did not seem to be helping the fate of their imprisoned compatriots, who were still being treated like animals. From news transmitted by the BBC, we learned that we could possibly be liberated by the Russians, yet our guards took pleasure in telling us that every one of us would be shot to prevent that.

As spring gave way to Summer 1944, it became evident that the Allies would have to invade, otherwise the Russian army would occupy the whole of Germany, and there was no way this could be allowed to happen.

I had only been physically assaulted by the Italians, never in the short time since I was taken to Stalag Luft 6 at Hydekrug, and so I was under the misapprehension that the Germans were more humane and would not ill-treat their British prisoners in any way. I learned differently. The first sign of it came when there was a commotion outside one night and a door was flung open by a guard. He did not need to push in his dog… it bounded in snarling and made in the direction of a bloke who was standing near his bed, three tiers of it. I swear that he reached the top unaided and without touching the other two, and remained there looking scared out of his wits. I never discovered what had provoked the guard's behaviour – maybe he had drunk too much schnapps.

Another incident that turned nasty was strange, to say the least. An aircraft was passing overhead, not close, but well within sight and quite noisy. This was unusual because we had not seen any for months, and all eyes were on it when the noise stopped… and the plane nose-dived. There was quite an explosion, at which we all cheered wildly. This was too much for the guards in the towers who started shooting, and it looked as if there would be wholesale slaughter, presumably ordered by their senior officer. Our terror was short-lived, however, as soon as we realised that the bullets were passing well overhead… but we had learned one of the most important unwritten laws – *Do not cheer when a German aircraft crashes!*

At last the long-promised secret weapon had materialised – the doodlebug – and only the fastest of our aircraft could engage them. Although it was now obvious that Germany had no hope of victory, the next period was to be the most savage that I had experienced.

Presumably because the Russians were coming too near for comfort we were driven like cattle into railway wagons, transported to Memel and loaded onto a tramp steamer, where I was expected to keep an eye on Bobby – the deranged prisoner – whose crippled mental state had, if anything, deteriorated. The confusion around us was such that I had no idea of who was there and what was actually going on; the guards at the camp had seemed to be older men, but these were different, younger men. So many prisoners were packed into the holds of the ship that it was 'standing room only' and some were even forced to climb on top of others. It is surprising what a prod from the tip of a bayonet can do!

I was left on deck with my charge, no advantage really, because there was no shelter, but luckily the weather was good. I remember looking down into the hold as we made our way to the rail to relieve ourselves, and it was like gazing into a snake pit, with bodies squirming around like serpents. It was hot, but we were wearing very little – all we had left to wear, in fact.

Water was difficult to come by, but the guards were lowering water in buckets so that the prisoners had to climb on top of each other to reach it, then emptying it over their heads. Bobby had seen this, and I noticed his mostly blank expression change to one of incredulity. Apparently thinking that he was seeing things, hallucinating, or perhaps believing that he was next in line to be so tortured, he rushed to the rail before I could stop him and jumped overboard. An ack-ack gun was fired at him. I could do nothing.

After disembarking we were pushed into cattle trucks and, although I had some boiled potatoes in a tin, from a Red Cross parcel, we were packed so tightly that I couldn't move my arm enough to get at them.

Our journey ended at a railway siding littered with empty cigarette packets and papers and several machine guns... which were trained on us. It looked as if we were to be massacred there and then, but they shackled us with leg irons. We did not know what to think, but the machine guns could easily have coped with the three to four hundred of us, all in very poor shape. I feel no shame in admitting that we were petrified with fear.

Onto the scene marched a company of soldiers. From a distance they did seem rather young, and as they came nearer it was clear that they were members of the Hitler Youth, the infamous movement launched by Hitler to train teenagers in the ways of warfare. They were known to show no mercy in any eventuality. An order was given which made them fix bayonets, then several dogs were released and, as we tried to get away from them, the soldiers (how could these fresh-faced boys be called soldiers?) charged at us and bayoneted as many as they could reach... which was not difficult since our legs were chained. The obvious thing was to get into the middle of the crowd, but of course this wasn't possible for everyone, and many prisoners were savaged.

I later helped to dress a man's back with over twenty wounds in it. A wound of this sort is unmistakable, as the blade leaves a pursed-lips appearance when it is pulled out. I don't know how far we ran – if you can call stumbling at each step running – until we saw the barbed wire. It seemed to be a camp, which had been built quite recently, and as we passed through the gates, there was a body search. I had no offending items on me, but a priest in front of me was beaten to the ground with the butt of a rifle for attempting to conceal a piece of soap.

It took a while to settle into our new abode and I have no knowledge of where it was situated. We learned that the British and Americans were pushing towards Germany and that Russia was making dramatic advances from the east. I felt sure that we would be shot... would *have* to be shot to hide the atrocities that had been perpetrated.

The winter of '44 was quite severe, which seemed to suit the Russians. Christmas passed and it was now becoming apparent that, if we were not moved again, and quickly, the camp would be overrun by the Russian Army. Needless to say, we were absolutely starving from lack of food and Red Cross parcels did not seem to exist here.

The move came in February 1945, when we had to take what we could carry (which in all cases was very little) before we started on the marches, escorted by numerous guards. We covered about fifteen miles each day and, in the initial stages, some sort of shelter was provided. During these days, in the crowd, I met up again with Rasmussen and Mason. Conditions were truly atrocious, not surprising really, I suppose, given the circumstances – we were simply refugees.

Obviously, few of us were accustomed to the rigours of this life, and cold wet feet did nothing to help. As for the rest of our bodies, what was left of them, we simply had to leave it to the wind to dry off. We became more or less inured to this, but how could one get accustomed to feet that were being numbed by the cold ... slowly being deprived of all feeling? In this bedraggled state, however, something strange happened to me... my feet had become pleasantly warm. It didn't make sense – frostbite possibly, but what was the source of the heat? Never mind the questions, I scolded myself, just enjoy it.

The pleasure was short-lived. Some of the blisters, which I had unknowingly acquired along the way, had burst, and the magic fluid was sloshing around in my boots. I was getting in a bit of a mess and the only respite was an occasional seat in the snow... but worse was yet to come.

My left leg was stiffening and a few miles farther on, the knee-joint locked. I was falling behind the others, which was attracting the attention of the guards, who were little better off than us and had no means or intention of interfering. It was the leg I had injured at the time of my capture, but I was almost ashamed to mention it. So many more were finding it impossible to keep going. Wounds which had been neglected or thought to be minor were now becoming life-threatening. I know that some fell by the wayside.

To give the impression that all this happened in silence would be utterly wrong, but the 'cheeky chappies' of earlier days were somewhat muted now. Emotions were stirred at seeing how many came to the aid of a comrade who was failing when they themselves were exhausted.

We made a stop at Lamsdorf, where the prisoners from Arnhem were held. They were very bitter at what had resulted from the parachute attack they had been ordered to make, and convinced that they had just been sacrificed. While there, though, I did manage to get hold of a tattered coat.

Weakness from hunger and the biting cold was getting the better of us – nights were spent lying in snow-covered fields, and death would have come as a mercy.

It was on one such night that Rasmussen, huddled close beside me, said, 'I'm going back to meet up with the Ruskies, Jock. They'd have been well prepared before advancing this far, so they're bound to have plenty food and warm blankets.'

'Don't be a bloody fool, pal,' I told him. 'You don't know how far behind us they are, nor what direction. You'll never survive out there on your own.'

'Probably not,' and I could hear his grin in his voice, 'so why don't ya come with me? If we stay with this lot, our life expectancy will be just a matter of days.'

I shook my head. 'No, we're better here. More than likely, the Reds will overtake us, and they're our allies. They can't turn their backs on us; they'll look after us.'

'They'll have transport, though. They'll make sure we get back to our own mobs.'

'It's no use, pal,' I muttered. 'They won't want to take prisoners at a time like this. They're set on reaching Berlin first, so…' I broke off, then pleaded, 'Don't go, you'll just be committing suicide.'

'You're not coming with me? That's your last word?'

'That's my last word.'

His sigh was long and ragged. 'Please yourself then, but I'm going back… with or without ya, Jock.'

We said our goodbyes crouching behind a wall to shelter from the steadily falling snow… and we clutched each other warmly before he walked away.

When the sun was shining, a faint ray of hope arose in the breast, a feeling that this purgatory could not go on forever.

How could God, if He were as wonderfully good as preachers made out to be, allow this to happen? Allow any of the atrocities of war to happen? It seemed that He was making no distinction between us and the enemy, treating us, in fact, worse than He was treating *them*. The British War Department would never allow German prisoners-of-war to be forced to undertake such a journey, underclad, underfed, under-everything, as we were; not in any circumstances. Strength and vitality had long since given way to a stubborn determination to survive. We *would* win through, whatever happened, whatever we had to face in the future. We British and our Allies could take it… couldn't we?

This hope, this certainty, did not last long in most cases; logic (as we thought) told us that to the Germans *we* were the enemy. They would be praying for victory as much as we were, praying to *their* God… to *our* God. Or was there no truth in the belief that God was omnipotent? Was there more than one God? Apart from the Gods of other religions, did each nation have its own Creator, Saviour, all-encompassing Being? If this was so, there was really no point in praying. We should just allow the Gods to fight it out between themselves – and may the best man (?) win.

These, and other ridiculous thoughts danced about in our heads, day after agonizing day, week after demoralising week, our moods depending on so many things. The sun, as I have already said, gave us a desperately needed boost. In dry, sunless weather, we could just about manage to convince ourselves that the Axis would be defeated soon, that all prisoners would be released… This was followed by the fear that, being on a march like this, probably out of range of any communication, our guards would not learn of capitulation when it came, and would lead us, those of us who were still fit to be led, right across Europe, out of Germany, through

France, Spain and Portugal, until, with nowhere else to go, they would expect us to follow them like lemmings into the Atlantic Ocean.

It was even worse when the skies were overcast, or when drizzling rain worked its way right through our pitiful clothes. It was at times like these that hope was practically an unknown quantity and imagination took another step down the Road to Despair. Our guards were not stupid. They must have some idea of how the war was going, and as soon as they learned that the end for Germany was imminent, they would shoot the lot of us. It would not matter that they were so outnumbered. We were unarmed and unable to fend off any attacks. They would easily finish off every last one of us. Even if those at the rear of the straggling column turned to flee when they realized what was happening they would not get far. They would soon be mown down like the rest of us…

Worst of all, of course, were the days when the rain came down in torrents – day after day of dragging our drenched bodies, our few clothes leaden with water, through a solid mass of mud, having to exert all our remaining strength at each step to free our feet from the suction which threatened to drag us down. At such times, wretchedly hopeless, we actually wanted our escorts to shoot us, wanted it all to end. No more of this draining effort. No more life-threatening hunger. No more of anything… just oblivion.

Then, thankfully, the rain would stop, the sun might make a belated appearance … and on we would go again.

Snow and ice were not the bogey that might be expected. Snow, although wetting to a certain extent, was not so cruel as the battering rain, and frost, of course, made the ground hard and easier to walk on. Ice posed a bit of a problem, but if we took it cautiously, we had fewer tumbles.

And, as winter gave way to spring, with more sightings of allied aircraft, we could actually begin to hope that our ordeal was coming to an end. Beyond that, we could not think. We could not foresee how we would be freed from the shackles which, although not there in actual fact, held us together as firmly as if we were in chains.

Surprisingly, even on this long, soul-destroying trek, there were lighter moments, such as the time that a horse-drawn cart with a load of bread was driven through the column of prisoners, none of us having eaten anything for days. Not much of its cargo survived to reach its intended destination! A few days later, Mason even exchanged his beloved gold watch for a few of the precious loaves. We ate ravenously.

At night we could hear the sound of aircraft and I could recognise the purr of a Rolls-Royce engine. Could it be possible? On another occasion we had been herded into a Dutch barn, just a roof, and had been trying to get some sleep – not just sleep, we prayed for utter oblivion – and it came some time in the night … the unmistakable sound of a Mosquito! Canon shells were ripping through the roof of our 'shelter'. Some of my companions were killed, and I can remember lying prone and pushing my face hard down into the earth.

The sound faded then returned even louder, and a rocket blasted the barn into blazing bits. We ran in all directions. I was alongside another prisoner when a shell hit him in the chest, blowing him apart. I collapsed into a ditch and must have lost consciousness.

The pain caused by a prodding bayonet brought me round. 'Rous! Rous!' a guard was shouting, but why he didn't just pull the trigger of his rifle, I will never know. So many had died.

Apart from turnips, and sometimes beet, from the fields, I can recall only one occasion when I got food, and that was when a cow was slaughtered. Germans do not eat offal, so I managed to get a piece of liver, which I wolfed down... raw. The thought of this may turn your stomach in these days of plenty, but when your whole body is weak from hunger, you are glad of the least little morsel... of anything.

Things were getting desperate when it was announced that there was to be an issue of parcels after we crossed the river we were approaching. No one believed it, there had been countless previous empty promises made, but we were ferried across in batches of about twenty, and sure enough, there were parcels waiting for us – not one each, just one between four... but manna from heaven, just the same.

It was shortly after this that I saw a formation of Flying Fortresses leaving trails of vapour behind them as they shot across the sky. What a sight that was! But we could not openly display our joy. The prisoners had, for some reason, been split into two batches at a Y junction, and we must have looked a pitiful lot – boots worn out, some even replaced by filthy rags, clothing caked with dirt, faces not washed or shaved for weeks. Lice, too, were becoming a problem, particularly in the crotch, and it was quite common to see someone sitting with testicles in hand burning off the lice with a piece of hot wood ... or a cigarette if he was lucky enough to have any. I must admit that cigarettes were usually obtainable from Canadians or Americans, who, in better times, had received thousands of them.

Shattering our short spell of welcome tranquillity one day, there came the roar of an aero-engine. It looked like a Typhoon, but I later learned that it was a Tempest. It was diving on the other column of prisoners, which was no more than two hundred yards away from ours. Make no mistake, these machines are purely for destruction! Despite the huge number of Allied prisoners who were killed or wounded in the mistaken belief that they were the enemy, the marches continued. I learned later that many were buried in a local cemetery.

Dysentery was an increasing problem, and with the lack of food, it didn't take long to become overpowering. For those who fell by the roadside, there was no hope.

As we travelled on, there was another tragic scene being enacted – refugees. I still don't understand why they were going eastwards while we were going west – I have no idea of their nationality, but they were either very old or very young, those least able to fend for themselves. God forbid that you should ever see such a sight, because I still find it hard to think of. Several of us tried to give them what we had but the guards threatened to shoot us if we did. These people, like us, were dirty – extremely dirty.

It was not like it is pictured in the cinema or television nowadays, even newsreels cannot put across the full horror of people forced to flee their homes and often their country during war. I never cease to admire those who, even today, risk everything to help refugees all over the world.

Aerial activity was increasing, and it was soon common to see Allied bombers overhead. This gave us a reason for living, but we were under no misapprehension. We knew we couldn't last much longer. The treatment varied. Even aware that Germany had very little chance now of winning the war, they still had faith in a secret weapon – a last-minute miracle taking place.

It was April, and even though the weather was less cruel, constant hunger was sapping any strength that remained. It did not help when I saw an aircraft travelling at what I estimated to be twice the speed of any Spitfire – a Messerschmidt 262. I only hoped that they didn't have many of them.

It was just another day when the thump of gunfire was suddenly all around us. The RAF was beating up an airfield only about a hundred yards away. That was too near, so I looked for a ditch and jumped in, out of sight. It transpired that the Luftwaffe was desperately short of aviation spirit and either could not take-off or did not want to commit suicide, so their aircraft were all on the ground, but our fighters quickly made sure that not one serviceable plane remained. Such is the power of air supremacy. To this day, I have little idea where all this happened. All I know is that it was a nice day and, at the time, the march didn't seem too bad. Can human beings get accustomed to anything?

I lay on my back to sleep. I was sure that I heard heavy artillery, albeit in the distance, and I thanked God for being alive. Could it be that I was a mere twenty miles or so from Allied artillery... or was it German? Exhaustion brought sleep, and in the morning, I was awakened by an unfamiliar noise – shouts of glee! The guards had fled and there was actually a tank in our midst, a British tank!

I could scarcely believe my eyes.

An officer who must have been the tank commander approached and handed me a bottle of whisky, but, unfortunately, we weren't able to drink such strong spirits. I only wish that I could have thanked him, but he was gone in a flash and I was left standing there, dazed, holding the whisky.

Events moved fast after this. We were taken to an army field kitchen, and I was well at the back of the queue for breakfast. There was bacon, eggs and bread, the like of which I had not seen before, and the bread, being white, was exquisite! I suppose that I did have more than one breakfast, and I can hear that Cook-Sergeant yet.

'Sorry, lads. The MO says I've to stop serving you. Your bellies will have shrunk and you won't be able to digest it if you eat too much.'

I can't recall what happened then, it's all rather confused now… it was more than sixty years ago, after all.

The soldiers were of the 6th Armoured Brigade, and they had more to do than attend to us. A nearby farmer, who was quite willing to see us die and had refused, before the advent of our 'saviours', even to give us water, was apparently pointed out – I'll say no more, but these men had recently liberated a concentration camp, so you can imagine how they were feeling. We struggled on, not really able to grasp what was happening, but at least we were getting something to eat.

My last encounter was nearly fatal. On entering a village, we were confronted by a Russian soldier carrying a machine gun. How he got there is a mystery, but he was hopelessly drunk and levelled the weapon at us. God, I thought, not now! Not after all we've been through!

I remember shouting, *'Tovarich!'* (the word that I had learned years ago) and pointing to my rather bedraggled flying brevet. It got through to him… just in time, and he lowered his gun.

I suppose we can't blame the Russians for getting whatever revenge they could, but the addition of alcohol to anger made a deadly mixture. I did have a sort of conversation with an officer who spoke quite good English, which was lucky, because my Russian consisted of only that one word that I am convinced saved my life.

'What happens now?' I asked him.

I was amazed to hear him say, 'We will shoot them.'

Thinking that I had heard him wrongly, I queried his calm remark, and he told me that a long time before, men had been conscripted from Mongolia and told to go west. They had done so with horrific casualties, and their one ambition was to slaughter as many Germans as possible. In this atmosphere, I managed to acquire a rifle from a deserted gun shop, which made me feel much better.

Out of the chaos came British soldiers who were to guide us to an encampment in preparation for taking us back to Britain, and the first thing they did was line us up for delousing, shaking copious quantities of DDT powder up the sleeves, down the collar and into the trousers – enough to keep us going until we reached the camp, which I was told was near Hanover, and where we did eventually arrive.

The Russian and Allied armies joined up amid great emotional scenes – it takes time to appreciate freedom to the full – and it was in this confusion that I learned that Germany had capitulated to Field Marshal Montgomery. Victory in Europe! VE Day! Although this was what we had prayed for, especially since being captured, we had come so close to giving up all hope of survival that we found it difficult to take in. What registered more with us then, was the large number of tents we could see, and we lost no time in getting down thankfully on the palliasses provided. It was a fitful sleep, however, waking frequently, unable to come to terms with the fact that the horror was really ending.

BACK TO NORMALITY

229 Squadron
R.A.F.
M.E.F.
14ᵗʰ June 1943

Dear Mrs Davidson,

You will no doubt have heard by now the official news regarding your son.

"Jock", as he was known to us all in the squadron, had been out on a show over enemy territory. On returning to base the section with which he was flying attacked enemy aircraft, but when the section reformed "Jock" was not to be seen anywhere.

"Jock" was very popular in the squadron and we shall miss him very much. He was above the average as a pilot and showed great keenness.

His effects are being dealt with by a standing Committee of Adjustment, who will communicate with you in due course. If, however, there is anything I can do for you please let me know, as I will be only too pleased to help.

I am enclosing his flying badge, which you may like to keep.

Yours sincerely
White
S/LDR.

The letter my mother received from Squadron Leader White

HOME AT LAST

The trip back to Britain in the bomb bay of a Lancaster on the 12th of May was uneventful, but it still hadn't quite sunk in that we were free. We were somewhat bewildered, having been repeatedly told by the Germans that we would be shot rather than allowed to be released, and knowing full-well that if they'd had the chance they would not have hesitated about carrying out their threat.

Many years were to pass before I could come to terms with a fear of fire. I would even wake in the night, imagining that I was engulfed in flames, with smoke pouring under the door – I could even smell it! I was scared to sleep in any room that was more than one storey up, and even then I would look out a rope to escape. Nightmares were almost nightly. I would be tramping on bits of bodies, then standing in front of a firing squad. The psychological strain was hard to bear, as it became more and more difficult to differentiate between dream and reality.

But enough of that! We were home at last, at RAF Melksham in Wiltshire... with my rifle. There was a full medical inspection, which showed that I had lost three and a half stones in weight, and then I was told that I was fit to go home, all within a day of our arrival! I was kitted out and given a rail warrant to Aberdeen... on indefinite leave.

It was a very emotional homecoming and Mother showed me the telegram which had told her that I was missing, also the letter from Squadron Leader White trusting that the worst had not happened. She must have been demented with worry until they let her know I had been taken prisoner, and I could tell that seeing me back home again was, for her, like a happy ending to a gruesome fairytale.

In case you are wondering – yes, I did go out 'on the town' when I felt a little better. I had met Alfie McDonald again – with whom I had tried to join the Gordon Highlanders and finished up in the Scottish Horse – and I also contacted friends from my engineering days with J.M. Henderson. Our favourite watering hole was the Athenaeum Hotel in Castle Street, which was selling a new beer called Double Diamond, quite strong ... perhaps a little too strong for my still delicate constitution. I took great delight in simply walking the streets, familiarising, reacquainting, myself with places I had almost forgotten, but I certainly did not forget to revisit Hazlehead Park and the other haunts of my boyhood.

I became very friendly with a local lass for a time. You may wonder why I did not try to get in touch straight away with Margaret Mackay, the girl I'd been seeing just prior to the outbreak of war, but we had both been little more than children then. In any case, it had seemed to me that she had not been altogether enamoured with the advances I had made to her at that time. Even after all I had been through, after all the humiliation and degradation I'd had to suffer, I still had a modicum of pride.

Although I was glad to be home, there came a point when I started to think of some way to get around more – perhaps I was getting too accustomed to seeing all the 'old places' – but the car that I fancied was rather expensive, away out of my league. *Nil desperandum*, however. I had truly enjoyed myself on the army motor cycle, and what was wrong with that as a personal vehicle? I didn't set out to go from place to place searching for something suitable, it was pure luck that I happened to spot a machine in the showroom window of

Cheyne's in Holburn Street … a Triumph Speed Twin in red and chrome décor. It was a real beauty! An eyecatcher!

The Twin was superseding most bikes of the time, and with my knowledge of things mechanical, its specification was very attractive. The cost, £159, had me pondering, though, but the more I turned it over in my mind, the more attractive it became. Back I went and told the proprietor of the shop that I was interested in buying. To my amazement, he told me that this was the first one he'd had, and because of the numbers of people it was drawing inside his showroom, he would like to retain it as an advertisement. As I still had to go back to Melksham to be demobilised, we arranged that I would collect it on my return.

My stay in Melksham was quite short, but the realisation that I was leaving the RAF was uppermost in my mind. It was such a big step, such a big decision, that I can recall being in two minds about signing on again.

It was a long, long journey from Wiltshire to Aberdeen and, as the trains were inevitably overcrowded, I was not looking forward to it. I don't know why; I had often travelled on crowded trains, even railway wagons. But it was great to be home… for good.

Yes, I bought the Triumph.

Around this time, I saw quite a lot of Alfie, my old pre-war chum, and was not at all surprised when he asked, one day, 'Will you give me a run to Tarland?'

I, of course, was quite happy to show off my Triumph, but curiosity made me ask, 'What's so special about Tarland?'

'I want to discuss things with one of the Land Girls,' he told me, sheepishly.

I grinned knowingly. 'Enough said, Alfie.'

When we reached our destination, I left him to sort things out with his girl, and while he was thus engaged – whether discussing past bloomers or future anxieties, he kept to himself – I met the farmer.

Although a Canadian, he had served in the British Army throughout the Great War and had been awarded the D.C.M. I took an instant liking to Alex and his wife Jean, and over a cup of tea, he asked me if I had been in the war. Not the Great War, naturally. When I gave him a summary of my varied service in the Scottish Horse, Royal Artillery and the Air Force, and the last two years as a prisoner in Germany, he was most impressed, and a close friendship was cemented. He stressed that I'd be welcome back any time, which invitation I gladly took up many times.

Alfie never told me where he and his friend had got to, or what conclusion had been reached, but he seemed very thoughtful when he appeared again. It was difficult to converse on a speeding motor cycle, which suited both of us on the way home.

Spring moved into summer in what was almost a fantasy, and I found myself thinking more and more of Margaret Mackay, yet I did nothing about it. What I knew about her, which was really very little, suggested that she would most likely be in the Services, yet my longing to see her again was tempered by a reluctance to hear that she had married – which she must be, by this time. But… while there's life, etc… and ridiculous as this seems, I decided not to commit myself to anyone until I met her again and found out if I'd any chance at all with her.

It was autumn before I heard from the RAF that I was to report back to Melksham, where a pleasant surprise awaited me. My rank since leaving Hawkinge had been established as Warrant Officer Class 1. I was kitted out accordingly and my spirits soared when I realised that my back pay would be fairly substantial.

But there was a decision to be made and I could not make up my mind what to do. First, I thought I should stay on in the Air Force; I even signed papers to this effect, yet everything was so different. It almost felt that I was back in the army, as there were uniforms everywhere. Then I heard a rumour that demobilisation was being accelerated for aircrews, of which there was now such a large number surplus to requirements that even the rapidly-growing civil airways could not incorporate those the RAF did not need.

My Group number was 27 on Class A release, and having been a POW meant that several options were still available to me, including immediate release. Because we were well paid, it was apparently thought that it would be difficult to get any of the aircrews to accept demobilisation, but as weeks passed, this proved to be untrue. At the end of my eighty days' leave and return to Melksham, it was evident that many had opted to go back to Civvy Street.

But the disease of flying was still with me, and I was somewhat taken aback when told that I was to be interviewed by the Group Captain. He looked at me quite understandingly. 'I believe that you are in two minds about leaving the service, and I thought it my duty to let you know that there are still a few good opportunities for fighter pilots with operational experience. The RAF does not want to lose such men.'

I don't know what came over me, but I had the impertinence to say, 'I'll consider staying in, sir, if I'm posted to an operational squadron.'

His answer was politely firm. 'In that case, I am sorry. The re-training you will have to undergo will not be justified unless you commit yourself by signing on.'

And that was that, although I was still quite bewildered when I left.

I had achieved ambitions far beyond my wildest dreams, and served with men with whom I am proud to have associated – I salute those who did not return – but after much deliberation, I accepted demobilisation. With it, of course, came the problem of finding employment.

As the entry in my RAF Service and Release Book shows, I had expressed an interest in becoming a policeman, probably because I hoped it might mean that I'd be able to fly again. It was a fact that serving police officers were accepted in the RAF Reserve. I soon decided to take the plunge and would apply to Aberdeen City Police.

I was appointed as a constable in March 1946. I was quite prepared to accept the discipline, and found many features similar to the RAF. I could not, however, abandon the nuts and bolts of my youth, and it wasn't long before I started to take an interest in model engineering, and bought a Myford turning lathe. But the war had left its marks. I still had a horror of fire, and sleepless nights.

I was back at square one, a Constable on Probation No.47. The training was quite intense and I was one of the first postwar entry to a force that was highly regarded in police circles. My priorities now had to be criminal law, road traffic regulations, police discipline procedures… and settling down at home, the order of these depending on the time of day or night.

There were times, of course, when I did have time to think of other things. Had I made a mistake in leaving the Air Force? I couldn't take my eyes off any aircraft passing overhead… wishing that I was in it, although the planes were different from the old days. The jet engine was well established now and it was the Meteor and the Vampire – much faster, almost projectiles – but the Spitfire could *fly!*

I did not care much for the police tunic, buttoned up at the neck and rather itchy; not to be compared with the fine material of my RAF tunic. The helmet was somewhat weird, but it was quite a few years before that style was abolished in Aberdeen.

Beyond the confines of the classroom, we started to get to know each other. Tales were told of previous lives and, as I remember, there was a bit of everything. Many were tradesmen; some, like me, had left the Services, while others had just completed their studies at university. A motley lot!

'Where do you come from?' or 'What did you do?' were, I suppose, the most common openings to conversations. I seemed to be the only one in that class who had been a prisoner-of-war. In spite of our meritorious services, the war was not a favoured topic of conversation, although it did come to the fore on occasions if criticism was misdirected.

On completing the course we were unleashed on an unsuspecting community – but not alone. A senior constable accompanied us, to 'show us the ropes'. Knowing the streets was one thing, but we were now expected to know them in minute detail, every lane and byway. If someone were to ask for directions to such-and-such a place, we couldn't say that we didn't know. That was one of the reasons for us being supervised.

It was on one of the early street patrols that I had an exceptional stroke of luck. A rather striking girl was coming towards us, claiming my immediate attention… but it couldn't be! As I stared, hopefully, at this vision, there came a hint of recognition in the beautiful dark eyes, then a smile. My supervisor discreetly walked on ahead and, in the circumstances, there could be no shilly-shallying. I took the bit between my teeth and asked her – yes, it was Margaret Mackay – if I could see her later. I was on duty, in uniform, and people passing might have thought that I was pushing public relations a bit too far, but what did I care? We met again that night in Jeannie's Café in Richmond Street, quite a decent wee place and not expensive. I could at least afford a Knickerbocker Glory.

We had a lot of years to catch up on and I was delighted to learn that, far from being married and settled down, Margaret had been in the ATS since May 1942. In the Ack-Ack, would you believe!

I couldn't help teasing her when I heard this. 'So it was you that shot at my little Spitfire when I flashed unannounced towards the south coast? How could you?'

Probably I had been safer in Germany, because she had been stationed just south of London, more or less in the flight path of the 'doodlebugs'. I listened anxiously as she recalled, 'We got some warning when the V1s' motors cut, but not with the V2s. Nobody could predict where they'd land.'

We didn't dwell on this subject. Our joy at meeting was such that the war seemed a million years away, yet she'd been demobbed only a few weeks earlier.

It wasn't long until Margaret took me home to meet her Mum and Dad – a real gentleman, who, in later life, suffered from the effects of gas attacks in the first war – also her brother, Sandy, six years younger than herself, and her sister, Mildred, only twelve at the time. Some months later, I took her to Mid Stocket Road, proof of my good intentions. My mother and sister took to her straight away, as she did to them, so there were never any awkward moments with either of our families. In fact, they all became very friendly – as though they'd known each other for years and years.

Working the night shift was usually awkward, but it did give Margaret and me the chance to check that there were no intruders in her lobby at Rosemount Place. I remember that it was better when I was off duty and our goodnights could be more prolonged, although I had the unwanted knack of getting my feet mixed up with the milk bottles that had been laid there for the milkman to collect in the morning. What a noise *they* made – enough to rouse every household in the building!

Margaret in ATS uniform.

The Triumph was all that I had expected it to be, and I kept it for 10 years – perhaps a bit of a comedown from 1,000 h.p., but it was all 'mine own' and it got me around. My gear was an army despatch rider's coat, an excellent garment, and, believe it or not, my RAF escape boots, which, if you remember, were presented to me in Hawkinge by the pilots of 91 (Nigeria) Squadron, and which I had taken to Aberdeen for safe keeping before I was posted to Malta – thank goodness. Margaret looked rather neat in a white leather helmet – and not just in the helmet!

I suppose the West Coast of Scotland was the greatest attraction for us – so beautiful if the rain and clouds didn't spoil it, though maybe it was better after a short shower. Taking a bump or a humpbacked bridge at too high a speed, however, was quite frightening, particularly for my pillion passenger. The bike took off! The road wasn't all that far beneath us, but far enough. How Margaret managed to stay on and we avoided a serious accident, I just do not know. That was in Glen Sheil, and the experience taught me a lesson.

The Author and Margaret + bike in Cornwall.

Our sights were eventually set on Cornwall, St. Ives, where Margaret's brother Sandy had been living for some time. It took us a couple of days... but was well worth it! The beaches and the warmer weather were most acceptable, but not the shark and the weaver fish I must have stood on. I was swimming in the harbour when I heard a shout, 'Look out! There's a shark!' I saw it, about 10 feet away. It was a basking shark, quite harmless, but I didn't know that at the time.

The weaver fish was much worse. I was making my way across the sands when the pain hit me – nothing to be seen. The pain became intolerable and I was taken to hospital, where I was told that it could have been fatal.

Not in my case, I'm thankful to say.

I was getting to know my colleagues in the force better. Several had been in the RAF in the later stages of the war, under a regulation that allowed them to transfer, but only for aircrew duties. I was accepted as one of them and was very much impressed by their demeanour, but there were such things as 'Senior Constables', some more aware of their rank than others. You really had to prove yourself to them!

It took a while to get accustomed to the shifts, and, surprisingly, the 6 a.m. was the most unpopular.

My sister Ellen married in 1948 and moved to Dundee where her husband worked. She made frequent visits home, however, and so was never regarded as having entirely left the fold. My dear mother lived for many more years – a wonderful old lady presiding over a happy, enlarged, family.

Margaret and I had been 'going steady' for three years, and I was more or less settled in the Police with the promise of a good career ahead of me when I took stock of the situation. As far as I was concerned, only one thing would make life perfect, so I plucked up my courage, took the bull by the horns and proposed.

I'm glad to say that she accepted with no hint of hesitation, and Margaret and I became husband and wife on 16 June 1949. It was a big step to take, but one which I have never had cause to regret… and nor has she, she assures me.

A New Start

At Christmas 1945, a card arrived from Rasmussen – and I thanked God that he had survived. Typical of him, though, he had forgotten to include his address, thus preventing me from replying. As I should have expected, I received another card from him the following year, with the un-Christmassy message – 'Write, damn you, write!'

I wished with all my heart that I could – we had gone through such a lot together and been as close as brothers, closer than some, and I'd have loved to get in touch with him again. If only there had been some way to arrange to talk to him on the telephone, what a tonic it would have been just to hear his drawling voice again. Unfortunately, I had never known exactly what part of the USA he came from, and in any case, he would probably be married by this time and have set up house somewhere else on that vast continent. What I did know, and still appreciate to this day, was that we were two of the lucky ones.

Desperate to get in touch with him, I made several attempts to trace him, through the International Red Cross etc, but without success and so, frustrated and saddened, I was forced to give up.

I did go back to visit Alex Jamieson, and took Margaret with me. Out of the blue, he asked me, 'Do you like to shoot? There's a gun behind the door.'

Trying not to offend him, I asked, 'What would I be allowed to shoot?'

'I own the place,' he smiled, 'so you can have your choice. There's plenty of game and I'd like you to keep down the rabbits.'

When I admitted that I had my own rifle with me, duly registered and licensed, he was delighted – it was the weapon from Germany, a 6.5 mm Mannlicher Schoenauer. (I subsequently acquired a shotgun, but the rifle was handier for roe deer.)

Alex was still a good shot, and although I shot game of all kinds on his land over the years and, despite the fact that he and his wife were by no means affluent, he refused to take anything from me. There are, however, other ways of repaying such privileges, and we remained great friends until his death in 1980. Jean lived on for another few years, and we frequently visited her at her home in Tarland. Long before then, of course, we had exchanged our two wheels for four.

A few years after embarking on my new career, I had the opportunity of going on an Air Observation course. This consisted of guiding a police car, from the air, to intercept a supposed criminal. The flying was done, in my case, by an RAF Flight Lieutenant in a light aircraft. Because I was well acquainted with the north-east of Scotland, I did not find it too difficult, and I couldn't resist asking if he would let me take over. I explained that I did have some flying experience, emphasising that I would obey all instructions.

At 6,000 feet, he told me to fly straight and level, which is not as simple as it may appear if done to exact limits in such an aircraft, but I soon got the feel of it, and asked if I could do some aerobatics. He agreed, a little reluctantly I must admit… and then I was in my element! It was as though I had never stopped flying, and to be scrupulously honest, I don't think I ever have… not in my mind, at least.

Ironically, after we landed and were walking back to the flight hut, my companion observed, 'You know something? You should be in the Air Force.'

But where were the Messerschmitts and Focke-Wulfs? My mind went back to all of them, including the pilot who had shot me down and had later given me his chocolate ration. There came a realisation – much of the exhilaration had evaporated. I would still enjoy flying if I had the chance, but there would be no more 'Huns in the sun'. Yes, I could dive – but the bombs had well and truly gone.

A SECOND CAREER & BEYOND

I am not going into any details about my career in Aberdeen City Police (Grampian Police, as it later became) – it would too much resemble the dozens of books, films and TV programmes that abound at present, and would be out of place in this account. Suffice it to say that it lasted thirty satisfying, rewarding years, and I attained the rank of Inspector in 1968. I retired in September 1976, aware that I would miss all aspects of the job: the companionship of my fellow officers, the stress, the frustrations, even the harassment we frequently had to undergo… but I would be free to indulge in my favourite pastimes.

It will come as no surprise when I say that my hobbies for many years were in the great outdoors – fishing and shooting. I took a great interest in angling, using my turning lathe to fashion many kinds of lures, and I was the possessor of at least one good gun which was put to full use. Striding out with my faithful dog by my side was almost like being in heaven.

Although my advancing years have curtailed both these activities, I can still feel the pull of them. I think, perhaps, that I should explain here exactly why they will always be a part of me. I would imagine that most young men have an instinct to participate in some sort of sport. I was no exception. I happily played football in the winter and cricket in the summer – which was all I needed. I did know that Bill Clark, one of my police colleagues held a number of trophies for shooting, but it was not until he suggested that I accompany him to the Portlethen Gun Club that we got to know each other and I found myself becoming deeply interested.

The rifles were of .22 calibre on a 25-yard range, and I was encouraged by my life in the RAF, where shooting was one of the principles in 'lead-off'… whether to a clay pigeon or a Messerschmitt. It was a bit of fun.

Invitations to 'shoots' were very welcome, but it soon became quite obvious that I would need a gundog if I were to do any serious game shooting. Having made the acquaintance of several of the shooting fraternity and seen the dogs they owned, I bought a Labrador pup. Margaret welcomed him – she had been brought up with animals and had treasured memories of a special dog called Haig. As far as I was concerned, however, there could be only one name for this puppy. How could he be anything other than Rab? It was the only way I could pay my respects to my never-to-be-forgotten friend, my one horse power.

As we often shot separately, Bill decided that we really need a dog each, and he also acquired a black Labrador, which he called Bonz. The two got on very well until they had a dispute over food; the grass is always greener on the other side, sort of thing.

Bill Clark and the two dogs were frequently my companions on trips to Alex Jamieson's farm near Tarland to keep down the vermin, a service that was well appreciated.

Rab needed little training, as the instinct was there, and Bonz was similarly dedicated. On one occasion, I stopped my car at Bill's house and rolled down my window to shout to let him know I was there. Bonz bounded out first, took off from the pavement and sailed into the car through the open window. He was determined not to be left behind. What could you say?

Over the years, I had three Labs and a Springer Spaniel that turned out to be something of a disaster. Each of them stayed in what had once been a coal cellar off the scullery, but had not been used as such for years, not since we went all-electric. This little cubby-hole was quite warm, near the furnace, so they couldn't have had a better kennel. The Spaniel, however, bored with being on his own, must have got hold of a loose corner of wallpaper one night, and by morning had stripped much of the walls. There were no antics like that with the Labs.

I am sure that everyone thinks that his dog is the best in the world, but I can prove my claim by relating one of several outstanding incidents... On one occasion three or four of us were spread out at the edge of a wood to shoot pigeons as they came in. Several were shot, but I was not doing too well. Rab suddenly disappeared, and I guiltily presumed that he was bored with having nothing to do, but he returned in a few moments to lay a pigeon at my feet. I had still had not shot any, but the mystery was explained when he returned with another bird, but followed this time by one of the other members of the party, his face a picture of exasperation.

'That's the second pigeon your dog's stolen out of my game bag,' he sighed.

There's devotion for you!

It was not how many birds you shot that mattered, of course, and it was understood that a pheasant rising nearby would be left alone, particularly a hen.

This was in the late days of myxamatosis, so it was better to shoot a rabbit than to leave it to suffer, or infect others.

A farmer or landowner who would agree to leave a decent part of a wheat or cornfield uncut was a precious commodity. In return, a 'feed' during hard weather was obvious – and the occasional bottle.

I did not care for large shoots, though. They became more and more like an army exercise. Of the men Margaret and I were to meet, there was one gamekeeper that I must mention… Wattie, at Fintray. He was somewhat older than us, but was very active; it took a good one to keep up with him. The River Don runs through this area, so there wasn't much that he didn't know about fishing. As I got to know him better, I was able to make lures for him, which he greatly appreciated, for his income would have been very modest and lures could be quite expensive to buy. He did not care for drinking, although he was often offered a bottle of whisky.

'I'd rather have a pair of socks,' was his usual reply.

His dog at the time was a gold-coloured Labrador, and he was occasionally to host some of the gentry's animals in his kennels. When I went shooting with him, I was always impressed with his speed in getting off a shot.

He was also a bit of a joker. One day, when Margaret was in the vicinity, I heard him shout 'Jock!' His dog 'came to heel', and Wattie crouched down in the grass and gave a few laboured puffs. This was enough for Jock, who tore at some long grass until his jaws could hold no more, and took it back to his gasping master. Wattie took the proffered toiletries and went through the motions of adjusting his trousers.

Maybe this 'act' had taken a few rehearsals, but it was exuberantly, and most realistically, performed, by both man and beast. Apart from these capers, Wattie was well known as an excellent dog trainer. He died a number of years ago.

Apart from the shotgun, I still had the 6.5 rifle I had acquired in Germany, and I got great pleasure in accompanying deer stalkers, mostly engaged in culling hinds in the winter.

I often recall days in the hills tramping through deep snow to get a vantage point where a clean kill was possible. A wounded red deer is not a good advertisement.

Margaret and I celebrated our Golden Wedding on 16 June 1999, not an elaborate affair, but an occasion for a reunion with her brother and sister – Sandy driving all the way from

Cornwall, and Mildred flying over from Canada, taking less time than he on her journey. It was the first time all three of them had been together for fourteen years, which added to the enjoyment.

Also present, but certainly no less important, were our son Neil and his wife, Jennifer, and our grandchildren, Kristoffer and Rachael, who have kept us young at heart.

~ END ~

Golden wedding 1999.

These, then, are the memories I wanted to record, ranging mainly over one of the most traumatic periods in the history of the 20th century. They tell how I, an apprentice engineer, came to realise a dream that I had cherished since I was a young lad, and how I came to live through so many vastly differing experiences. I have purposely glossed over my work in the police, as I wanted to concentrate on the thirties and forties, and how my forces training influenced my choice of hobbies in my retirement. I hope that what I have written has made interesting reading.

Afterthought: According to a newspaper report, a recently-rebuilt Spitfire cost £1,000,000... I think I'll go back and dig mine up!

Nissen Hut at Huntly

Aircrew relaxing, Malta..

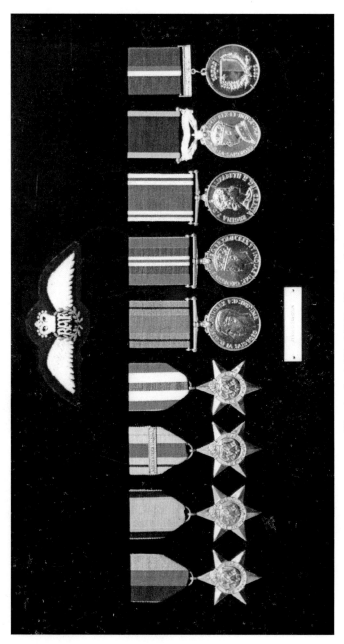

The Author's World War Two medals.